Tasting New Mexico

Tasting New Mexico

Recipes Celebrating One Hundred Years
of Distinctive Home Cooking

by Cheryl Alters Jamison
and Bill Jamison

Contemporary photography
by Sharon Stewart

Museum of New Mexico Press
Santa Fe

*For Riley, Bronwyn, and Chloe's generation
of New Mexico cooks and eaters*

Tiles courtesy Artesanos Imports Co.

Project editor: Mary Wachs
Design and production: David Skolkin
Manufactured in China
10 9 8 7 6 5 4 3

Library of Congress Cataloging-in-Publication Data

Jamison, Cheryl Alters.
  Tasting New Mexico : recipes celebrating one hundred years of distinctive New Mexican cooking / by Cheryl and Bill Jamison ; contemporary photography by Sharon Stewart.
    p. cm.
  ISBN 978-0-89013-542-6
(paperbound : alk. paper)
  1. Cooking, American—Southwestern style. 2. Cooking—New Mexico. 3. Restaurants—New Mexico. 4. New Mexico—Social life and customs. I. Jamison, Bill. II. Title.
  TX715.2.S69J357 2011
  641.59789--dc23
                            2011035277

Museum of New Mexico Press
PO Box 2087
Santa Fe, NM 87504
www.mnmpress.org

Contents

Introduction: One Hundred Years of Statehood, Thousands of Years of Living Food History

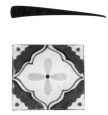

WHEN CHRISTOPHER COLUMBUS accidentally bumped into the Caribbean islands in 1492, he had no idea that historians would soon credit him for the discovery of the New World. His intended destination was the Malabar Coast of southern India, fabled since ancient times as the home of black pepper, a food seasoning so prized and pricey that some traders dubbed it "black gold." Columbus simply assumed that he had arrived in India, creating centuries of linguistic confusion by identifying the local people as "Indians" and their spicy chiles as a kind of pepper.

At the time, when Spain had a population of around five million, four times as many of these Indians lived in Central and North America. Equipped with superior weapons and horses, the Spanish conquered and subdued the natives everywhere they went, from the "West Indies" to Mexico, Peru, and, ultimately, New Mexico and other areas of the American Southwest. Over time they located and mined tons of precious metals, but more important in the long run they discovered a trove of foods unknown to the rest of the world. Particularly in the fertile central valley of Mexico, home of the Aztecs, the invaders found, among other edible treasures, chocolate, vanilla, tomatoes, and specially bred varieties of chiles, corn, squash, and beans, some of which had already made their way north to New Mexico as cultivated crops long before the Spanish arrived.

In most respects, agriculture was equally advanced in this period in the New and Old Worlds, with the Europeans having a major advantage only from the possession of livestock for meat and burdensome work. The colonists soon leveled the playing field in that regard, introducing cattle, hogs, horses, sheep, goats, and other domesticated animals everywhere they settled in the Americas.

Colonial Cuisine

The Spanish made several forays into New Mexico starting in 1539, less than twenty years after Hernán Cortés overran the Aztecs and founded New Spain. Little came of most of the *entradas*, as the Spanish called them, until Juan de Oñate brought permanent settlers north on a seven-month trek in 1598. The wagon caravan, which stretched more than two miles in length, carried around

500 colonists, 243 bushels of wheat, seeds for Aztec chiles and many European crops, more than 40 iron plowshares, plenty of chickens, and 7,000 head of livestock. The soldiers, officials and their families, and Franciscan missionaries—who together constituted the core of the party—didn't intend to do much farming themselves, but they counted heavily on local Indian labor to provide them with proper Spanish provisions. Unlike many European colonists on the Atlantic coast, who were often fleeing their mother country, these pioneers remained intensely loyal to their homeland and national heritage, including its culinary traditions.

In the words of William W. Dunmire, the preeminent horticultural historian of this time and place, "a mighty food pathway into the American Southwest—one that endured for three centuries—had been launched." First in Mexico and then in New Mexico, the Spanish and natives of the Americas forged one of the most dynamic blends of food cultures ever seen in human history. The Spanish contributed ingredients from the Mediterranean, more varied than those of England and northern Europe, and the natives taught them about the marvels of corn, chiles, and other delights destined for global renown.

Despite significant similarities, the cuisines of Mexico and New Mexico evolved differently. Mexico enjoyed greater culinary bounty with its tropical produce and seasonings, its access to the sea, and its more direct connection with Spain and the rest of the world. With these additional resources, colonial cooks in major urban areas developed a superbly sophisticated cuisine. Months away by wagon from Mexico and other European settlements, and in contact only occasionally, settlers in New Mexico evolved a more rustic, heartier cooking style featuring chiles as an essential, pronounced ingredient in many of the main dishes. Some New Mexico foods sound in name like ones from Mexico or other parts of the American Southwest, but a single bite usually shows the bold difference. Even without the extra assets of Mexico, New Mexico still participated broadly in the historic synthesis of Spanish and native food cultures and did so to a much greater degree than anywhere else in the future United States. The cooking grew in distinctive ways from the beginning and remains distinctive to this day.

Oñate's entourage settled at San Gabriel alongside Ohkay Owingeh Pueblo north of present-day Española. The first task was building an *acequia madre*, or mother ditch, to divert river water into planned fields, work carried out by more than a thousand conscripted Pueblo laborers. Wheat went into the ground first, befitting its importance in the Spanish diet, followed before long by chiles, barley, artichokes, cabbage, lettuce, carrots, garlic, onions, radishes, turnips, cucumbers, garbanzos, peas, plums, and cumin. Within a generation, the colonists also began raising fava beans, lentils, vetch, apricots, cherries, nectarines, peaches, apples, and wine grapes. Largely for themselves, but partially in tribute to the Spanish, Pueblo farmers in their own gardens grew corn, beans, squash, and cotton along with two Mediterranean fruits that had traveled up from Mexico before the Spanish, cantaloupe-like melons and watermelons. Anything people didn't eat fresh was dried for future meals during the winter and spring. Not everyone, by any means, benefited equally from the largesse, but after an initial adjustment period many of the Spanish ate well, at least by international standards of the day.

Predictably, the Spanish livestock didn't always thrive in the new environment. The San Gabriel settlers ate most of the cattle that accompanied them north, and the surviving herd never flourished in great numbers until much later. Pigs didn't adapt well to the arid climate and desert terrain, but colonists kept enough of them around to enjoy pork occasionally. Goats felt right at home from the beginning, and their milk provided fresh cheese for the colony. Churro sheep, prized for their wool as well as their meat, multiplied so rapidly that they became one of the earliest exports back to Mexico, and mutton was the protein of choice up to the turn of the twentieth century.

At San Gabriel a few disappointing harvests combined with internal strife encouraged the colonists to seek a fresh start a short distance south in Santa Fe, officially founded in 1610 though originally settled a little earlier. Around the same time, King Philip III declared New Mexico a royal colony of New Spain and decided that the primary purpose of the remote province should be the conversion of Indians to Christianity. In theory, few Pueblo and Diné (Navajo) residents objected to the notion, trusting that two religions might be better than one. The Franciscan missionaries, however, regarded the Indian beliefs as thoroughly pagan and set out to abolish them totally. This and other grievances—exacerbated by a long drought and thousands of native deaths from famine and diseases brought from Europe—led to the Pueblo Revolt of 1680 that drove the Spanish out of New Mexico for twelve years.

When the Spanish returned under the leadership of Diego de Vargas, they and the Puebloans gradually found accommodation with each other, even to the point of intermarrying with some frequency. The Spanish dropped demands for Indian labor and a halt to Pueblo religious practices, and began concentrating instead on establishing family homesteads and providing a distant military buffer to protect the heartland of New Spain in Mexico. The two groups also formed a strong common bond in dealing with increasingly widespread and deadly raids by nomadic Indian tribes and sometimes by the Diné.

Shortly after their return, the Spanish established new towns in Santa Cruz, Bernalillo, and Albuquerque, but during the rest of the colonial era population growth occurred mainly in outlying rural areas, particularly in mountain valleys, north around present-day Taos, east of Santa Fe, and south of Albuquerque toward what is now Socorro. The land-grant system tended to promote dispersion. Officials awarded some prominent citizens huge tracts of land to raise livestock, but most grants went in much smaller parcels to individual families or villages of farmers and herders.

The gradual expansion of settlement brought an increase in the range of food crops. The tomato arrived by 1745, and in the same period chroniclers first mention pears, quinces, and anise. Within another half century, some growers were planting rye, black mustard, and saffron. At this point, moving into the nineteenth century, New Mexico was more populous, strategically important, and better fed than any other future state in the American West, including the Spanish-settled lands of Arizona, California, and Texas.

When Mexico gained its independence from Spain in 1821, bringing along New Mexico as a passive partner, the historic break fostered opportunities for foreign trade and led promptly to the opening of the Santa Fe Trail. In the next few decades thousands of wagon trains crossed the storied route between western Missouri and Santa Fe, expanding the quantity of imported goods in New Mexico and making everything more affordable. What new foods and beverages did the Anglo traders introduce to our isolated capital? Nothing much except barrels of oysters and casks of French champagne. In the whole of the eastern and central United States there was hardly anything edible or drinkable that wasn't already available at some price in frontier New Mexico.

The trade benefited New Mexico cooks mainly by reducing the cost of many imported foodstuffs—items such as sugar, spices, chocolate, and rice—that had previously come up from Mexico on the Camino Real. Especially after the arrival of the railroad in 1879, traders also brought in a wealth of manufactured goods, including kitchen tools, farming implements, and an increasing array of packaged foods.

The kinds of dishes prepared in prosperous households during this period are known to a fair degree from writings of Anglo visitors who were invited to meals in Hispano homes. One gentleman told about a dinner in Bernalillo that started with a vegetable soup and also included roasted chicken, boiled mutton, beans, "the finest white bread," and ample wine made on the property. He went on to comment: "Chilé the Mexicans consider the chef-d'oeuvre of the cuisine, and seem really to revel in it; but the first mouthful brought the tears trickling down my cheeks, very much to the amusement of the spectators with their leather-lined throats. It was red pepper, stuffed with minced meat."

His initial reaction to chile was typical of visitors, but on the whole the longer they stayed, the fonder they became of New Mexico food. The experience of Susan Shelby Magoffin, the young bride of a trader and one of the first Anglo ladies to travel the Santa Fe Trail, illustrates the trend in detail because she took more careful and copious notes on food in her journal than most men did. Her initial meal in the village of Las Vegas, then poor and rural, appalled her. In reaction to the main dish, a stew of meat, onions, and green chile, she said, "we had neither knives, forks, or spoons, but made as good substitutes as we could by doubling a piece of tortilla, at every mouthful—but by the by there were few mouthfuls taken, for I could not eat a dish so strong, and unaccustomed to my palate." Perhaps puzzled by the problem, since locals would have regarded this as a fine meal, the hosts substituted fried eggs and roasted corn.

By the time Magoffin had her "first entire Mexican dinner" in Santa Fe, she had gotten more enthusiastic about the cooking. The dinner consisted of *sopa de fideos* (vermicelli in broth), a dish of buttered rice topped with slices of hard-boiled eggs, various kinds of roasted and boiled meats, a dessert that might have been *natillas*, and lots of champagne with every course. Continuing south toward El Paso, a New Mexico town at the time, she praised simple meals of tortillas and beans as well as fancier local fare in the homes of friends. Eventually, after several months, she decided, "I shall have to make me a [New Mexico] recipe book, to take home, the cooking in every thing is entirely different from ours, and some, indeed all of their dishes are so fine 'twould be a shame not to let my friends have a taste of them too." Before she had a chance to fulfill the pledge, Magoffin died in childbirth.

Pueblo, Diné, and Hispano families who depended almost entirely on self-sufficiency ate less meat than more affluent residents and didn't often have multicourse meals, but they usually enjoyed ample sustenance except in years of poor harvests. Most of the time they relied on corn rather than wheat for a grain, using it in tortillas as well as dishes brought up from Mexico such as tamales, posole, and the corn beverage called atole. In a further difference from upper-class families, they were also more likely to eat chile stews, vegetable dishes, and the precursors of what we now call enchiladas, tacos, and burritos.

Most Hispano adults, regardless of status and income, drank wine as frequently as possible. El Paso and Bernalillo both produced wines that colonists and Anglo traders alike lauded. Records from the period tell us that at the celebration of Mexican Independence Day in 1844, the refreshment committee for the evening fandango spent most of its budget on forty-three flasks of wine, although it also served pastries, puddings, candies, cookies, *aguas frescas*, and punch spiked with strong local brandy.

Anglo visitors often expressed surprise and sometimes disgust at the local fandangos. One experienced trader, Josiah Gregg, wrote: "To judge from the quantity of tuned instruments which salute the ear almost every night in the week, one would suppose that a perpetual carnival prevailed everywhere." Other travelers from the democratic United States displayed shock at the egalitarian nature of the frequent parties, which seemed to attract almost everyone in town, from priests to paupers, and featured unabashed dancing and mingling between men and women from entirely different social classes.

Enduring Food Traditions

In 1846, the same year Susan Magoffin toured New Mexico, the U.S. Army rode into Santa Fe and seized the province from Mexico. It was one of the opening acts in a war initiated in Washington, DC, to fulfill the nation's supposed Manifest Destiny of expanding to the Pacific Ocean. To the political leaders of the country, New Mexico was a small stepping-stone on the way to California, but the army remained a major presence in the area for another forty years, until Geronimo's final surrender ended the Indian wars in the Southwest.

Shortly after New Mexico officially became a territory of the United States, Anglos began arriving in increasing numbers in pursuit of various opportunities. Ranchers came from Texas to raise cattle to feed the army, and one of them, John S. Chisum, ultimately acquired a herd as large as any in the country on his Roswell spread. The railroad, another entrepreneurial attraction for Anglos, further stimulated the cattle trade, bringing New Mexico stockmen access to a national market that craved beef. Ranches and farms proliferated in the previously unsettled southern part of the territory, opening up the fertile Mesilla Valley for cultivation and making Las Cruces an important rail center. Hispano sheep ranchers in the north foresaw a dwindling demand for mutton, which wasn't nearly as popular as beef across the country, and also faced an overgrazing crisis in some areas; most of them gradually shifted their operations toward raising steaks.

Along with its promotion of cattle ranching, the railroad also increased access to pork raised in other areas, making it a more common, affordable meat that worked as well or maybe even better than mutton in traditional New Mexico dishes. Early-twentieth-century cookbooks hint at the evolution of tastes. For the New Mexican style of chile con carne, the first published recipes call for two pounds of mutton (or beef if preferred) plus one pound of pork, but they specify pork alone for carne adovada and posole stew.

Not all the opportunities sought by Anglos in the territorial period were as legitimate as ranching and railroading. The freewheeling frontier environment also lured ruffians, rustlers, and swindlers. Some of the most notorious figures became prominent civic leaders in the Santa Fe Ring, a group of polished thieves who prospered from political corruption and fraud involving Pueblo and Hispano lands.

When New Mexico attained statehood in 1912, the Santa Fe Ring still exerted some sway in the capital, but the tide of Anglo immigration was shifting. Artists, writers, and scholars were discovering the wonders of the state and began challenging the influence of people who came to take advantage of local conditions in one way or another. This band of enthusiasts may never have constituted a majority among the newcomers, but they spoke in a much louder and more passionate voice than anyone else. Devoted to historic and cultural preservation, they helped to establish the dominance of the Spanish Pueblo architectural style in Santa Fe, molded the state museum system in its early years, fought actively alongside Pueblo residents against the infamous Bursum Bill that would have undercut Pueblo property rights, and promoted a revival of Spanish colonial folk crafts.

In a lesser-known effort, two leaders in this group even took a strong stand on behalf of traditional Hispano and Pueblo cooking. Alice Stevens Tipton in *New Mexico Cookery* (1916) and Erna Fergusson in her *Mexican Cookbook* (1934) demonstrated bold initiative in favor of time-honored local foods at a point when every national culinary trend pointed in different directions. Tipton in particular insisted on the need to use New Mexico ingredients, being about a century ahead of her time in that respect. Neither book sounds anything at all like the work of Fannie Farmer, the most famous American cook of the day, who probably would have bolted from a dining table at the mere mention of chile.

The Tipton and Fergusson cookbooks were the first published in New Mexico after statehood, and they gave the earliest detailed descriptions of how to craft beloved historic dishes, including red and green chile sauces made from scratch, corn and flour tortillas, red cheese enchiladas with an optional fried egg, chiles rellenos, tamales, albóndigas (meatballs), flan, capirotada (Spanish bread pudding), and many other authentic preparations. Fergusson, also a noted historian, went beyond the recipes to include instructions for drying fruit the old way and making fresh goat cheese at home.

Shortly after the publication of these pioneering works, four influential Hispano ladies recorded their own recipes and recollections in important cookbooks. They knew that descendants of the colonial Spanish would soon no longer be a majority in the state, and they sought to encourage New Mexicans to protect their heritage and resist the temptations of American convenience foods. Margarita C. de Baca, daughter of a former governor, came out in 1937 with *New Mexico Dishes*, a comprehensive review of the subject. Cleofas M. Jaramillo, a founder of La Sociedad Folklórica de Santa Fe, followed two years later with *The Genuine New Mexico Tasty Recipes: Old and Quaint Formulas for the Preparation of Seventy-five Delicious Spanish Dishes*. In 1941, the owner-operator of one of the earliest New Mexican restaurants in the state, Santa Fe's El Plato Sabroso, Eloisa Delgado de Stewart presented her *El Plato Sabroso Recipes*, only twenty pages long but full of flavor. After World War II, in 1949, Fabiola Cabeza de Baca Gilbert released *The Good Life: New Mexico Traditions and Food*, based partially on a previous circular she wrote in her job as a home economist and extension agent. In contrast to this remarkable series of works, the single Anglo-American cookbook from New Mexico in the same period displayed similar skill and ardor only for cakes and other conventional desserts.

Together, these six ladies—with later help from Katy Griggs Camuñez Meek, Lucy Delgado, Ana Pacheco, Norma Naranjo, Rita Edaakie, and others—played a vital role in preserving and passing on the culinary traditions they loved. They inspired both restaurateurs and home cooks, creating momentum behind the food and providing continuity into the future. Whether you've read any of their books or other writings or not, if you cook New Mexican fare in your own kitchen or enjoy eating it out, you have been enriched by their efforts.

The same holds true for contemporary farmers who have revived family-scale agriculture and heirloom seed lines in the state. In 1940, right before America entered World War II, New Mexico had thirty-four thousand farms and ranches, many of them tiny mom-and-pop ventures. Within a decade, after the highest rate of war deaths of any state in the nation and steady migration from the country to cities, the number of small farms dropped substantially, larger operations grew considerably in acreage, and commercial agriculture reigned. This trend has moderated and even reversed to some degree in recent years as numerous families across the state have returned to the land, rescued crops not suited to mass production, and helped to create alternative sales venues such as farmers' markets. As a result the quality of locally raised food has soared.

As food goes, so goes culture. In Pueblo beliefs, corn is not only the staff of life but a sacred icon. In Hispano homes in New Mexico, food ways are folkways and Spanish words still denote everything dear. Cherished customs never have separate compartments.

In the one hundred years since statehood, New Mexico has certainly felt the major impact of American values and practices. In business, education, war, and almost all pursuits, New Mexico steps in concert with the other forty-nine states. At the same time, culturally it remains a land apart. The vast majority of Pueblo, Diné, and Hispano residents yield no ground on their most treasured traditions, and most of their Anglo neighbors today appreciate the dedication to heritage and look for chances to partake of its blessings. In the end, it's what makes us all New Mexicans.

Beekeeper, Cimarron, 1909-13.
Photo by Edward A. Troutman,
courtesy Palace of the Governors
Photo Archives (NMHM/
DCA), 149015.

Chile drying, Pueblo village,
ca. 1925–45. Photo by
T. Harmon Parkhurst, courtesy
Palace of the Governors Photo
Archives (NMHM/DCA),
005176.

Opposite, top: *Peppers drying, San*
Juan Pueblo, 1928. Photo by
Irving Galloway, courtesy Palace
of the Governors Photo Archives
(NMHM/DCA), 005143.

Opposite, bottom: *Shipping piñon*
crop, Gormley's General Store,
Santa Fe, 1916. Photo courtesy
Palace of the Governors Photo
Archives (NMHM/DCA),
014196.

SHIPPING 1916 CROP PINON NUTS
GORMLEY'S GENL STORE SANTA FE, N.M.

Cutting the pies and cakes at the barbeque dinner, Pie Town, New Mexico Fair, 1940. Photo by Russell Lee. Courtesy Library of Congress.

Right: *Maclovia Lopez cooking tortillas directly on the stove, 1943. Photo by John Collier, Jr. Courtesy Library of Congress.*

Left: *Cowboy cooking in chuckwagon, Bell Ranch in northeastern New Mexico, ca. 1940. Photo by Harvey Caplin, courtesy Palace of the Governors Photo Archives (NMHM/ DCA), 008532.*

Camp kitchen at the Los Alamos Ranch School, ca. 1935. Photograph by T. Harmon Parkhurst, courtesy Los Alamos Historical Museum Photo Archives.

Fuller Lodge dining room during the Manhattan Project, ca. 1945. Photograph courtesy Los Alamos Historical Museum Photo Archives.

Opposite, top: *Plaza Café, Santa Fe, 1947, on the day Dionysi (Danny) Razatos (left) bought the restaurant from his former boss, Mr. Pomonis, at right. Photo courtesy Andy Razatos.*

Opposite, bottom left: *La Fonda de Santa Fe menu, 1954. Courtesy Fray Angélico Chávez History Library (NMHM/DCA), 478-1.*

Opposite, bottom right: *Leona's, Chimayó, 2010. Photo courtesy the authors.*

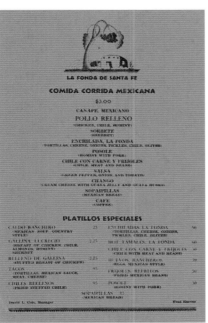

La Fonda de Santa Fe

COMIDA CORRIDA MEXICANA

$3.00

CANAPE MEXICANO
POLLO RELLENO
(CHICKEN, CHILE, PIMENT)
SORBETE
(SHERBET)
ENCHILADA, LA FONDA
(TORTILLAS, CHEESE, ONIONS, PICKLES, CHILE, OLIVES)
POSOLE
(HOMINY WITH PORK)
CHILE CON CARNE Y FRIJOLES
(CHILE MEAT AND BEANS)
SALSA
(GREEN PEPPER, ONION, AND TOMATO)
CHANGO
(CREAM CHEESE WITH GUAVA JELLY AND GUAVA BREAD)
SOPAILLAS
(MEXICAN BREAD)
CAFE
(COFFEE)

PLATILLOS ESPECIALES

CALDO RANCHERO (MEXICAN SOUP, COUNTRY STYLE)	.25	ENCHILADAS, LA FONDA (TORTILLAS, CHEESE, ONION, PICKLES, CHILE, OLIVES)	.40
GALLINA LUCRECIO (BREAST OF CHICKEN, CHILE, ALMONDS, PIMENT) SHERBET	2.25	HOT TAMALES, LA FONDA	.40
RELLENO DE GALLINA (STUFFED BREAST OF CHICKEN)	2.25	CHILE CON CARNE Y FRIJOLES (CHILE WITH MEAT AND BEANS)	.40
		HUEVOS RANCHEROS (EGGS, MEXICAN STYLE)	.30
TACOS (TORTILLAS, MEXICAN SAUCE, MEAT, CHEESE)	.35	FRIJOLES REFRITOS (FRIED MEXICAN BEANS)	.30
CHILES RELLENOS (FRIED STUFFED CHILE)	.40	POSOLE (HOMINY WITH PORK)	.30
		SOPAILLAS (MEXICAN BREAD)	.15

LEONA'S

HAND HELD BURRITOS!

ALL BURRITOS ARE MADE ON LEONA'S HAND MADE WHOLE WHEAT TORTILLAS!
CHOICES: RED OR GREEN CHILE
CHEESE SAUCE OR GRATED CHEESE
GUACAMOLE OR SOUR CREAM ----- .50 EXTRA

CHICHARRONE & BEANS	$4.95
CARNE ADOVADA	4.95
CHICKEN	4.95
CHICKEN & BEAN	4.95
ROAST BEEF	4.95
ROAST BEEF & BEAN	4.95
POLISH SAUSAGE BURRITO	4.95
TAMALE BURRITO	4.95
QUESADILLA BURRITO--CHEESE, CHEESE & CHEESE-	3.95
BEAN	3.95
VEGGIE--BEANS, LETTUCE, TOMATOES, ONIONS & CHEESE-	3.95
EGG--WITH POTATOES, CHILE & CHEESE--(BACON $1.00)	3.95

LEONA'S HOMEMADE TAMALES

PORK -- PORK MEAT & RED CHILE	$1.95
CHICKEN -- CHICKEN GREEN CHILE & CHEESE	1.95
VEGGIE -- ZUCCHINI, GREEN CHILE & CHEESE	1.95
VEGGIE -- ZUCCHINI & RED CHILE -- NO CHEESE	1.95
CHICKEN -- NO CHILE -- CHICKEN & CHEESE	1.95
DOZEN -- $17.00	

HOURS   11:00 - 5:00 PM

OTHERS

CORN ON THE COB	$1.95
TACO --------------bean 2.95--chicken 3.50	
HOT DOG	1.95
TOSTADA --------------bean 2.95--chicken 3.50	
NACHO CHEESE & CHIPS	3.50
SALSA & CHIPS	3.50
GUACAMOLE & CHIPS	3.50
CHICHARRONES (8 OZ. TUB)	3.95
BANANA BREAD	1.75
BISCOCHITOS	1.50
PANOCHA	1.75
CAPIROTADA--Bread Pudding	2.50
PEANUT BUTTER CLUSTERS	1.50

12 OZ. BOWLS

BEANS	$4.50
FRITO PIE	4.50
SPANISH RICE	4.50
POSOLE	4.50
TAMALE PIE	4.50
ENCHILADA CASSEROLE	4.50
CHILE STEW	4.50

COLD DRINKS
IN CUP WITH ICE

$1.25 -- $1.50 -- $1.75

COKE, DIET COKE, SPRITE, DR. PEPPER, ROOT BEER, ICE TEA, LEMONAIDE, SLUSHES

HOT DRINKS

$1.25 -- $1.50 -- $1.75
HOT COFFEE OR TEA
HOT CHOCOLATE
HOT/COLD CIDER
CAPPUCCINO

REFRIGERATOR

CAN SODA	$1.25
JUICES	1.25 & 1.75
BOTTLED WATER	1.75
GATORADE	2.00

CLOSED TUESDAYS AND WEDNESDAYS

The business of barbeque: Pete Powdrell with wife Catherine and sons Mike (left) and Joe, Albuquerque, 1991. Courtesy Joe Powdrell and New Mexico Magazine.

Authors' Apology for Leaving Out Your Favorite New Mexico Dish

WE DIDN'T DO IT DELIBERATELY. We don't even know what the dish is. But we're pretty sure that we're the only two people in the state who will agree a hundred percent with our selection of recipes to feature in the following pages. Frankly, that's exactly the way it should be when the subject is traditional cooking in any locale. We're thrilled that New Mexicans care enough about our shared foods that they will want to tar us with tomatoes, eggs, or even chiles.

We did have some criteria and some limitations. Since the book celebrates the state's centennial, we thought the vast majority of dishes should seem somewhat recognizable to a Rip van Winkle who awoke suddenly from a century-long sleep. We allowed only a few exceptions for dishes that have become widely popular since then and are based on flavors and ingredients that are a core part of our culinary heritage, fare such as green chile cheeseburgers and tacos. The beloved frito pie was left on the cutting room floor because of its emphasis on decidedly Texan Fritos corn chips. Looking broadly across the state and over centuries of time, the foods included here seem to us to best represent the long and proud heritage of New Mexico cooking.

We did let contemporary tastes affect our selections. A good friend of ours, a native New Mexican, ate baked goat's head as a child, and it wasn't considered unusual in his area of the state in the 1950s. We know the dish can be tasty, particularly the cheeks, but we couldn't see it on the menu at a modern centennial fiesta.

In terms of recipe details, all we can say is that we have to follow our own taste buds. We know each of the dishes in the book can be made in many different ways, and other cooks may be able to improve on our way of making some dishes. If you're lucky enough to have your grandmother's recipe for red chile sauce and it's the best you've ever eaten, please continue honoring her memory by cooking it. We have strived for two primary results in the recipes: simplicity in preparation steps to ensure broad accessibility and fullness of traditional flavor. Every recipe has been thoroughly tested by us in our home kitchen.

In short, for our omissions and our wayward deviations, we accept the blame, and we are elated that thousands of New Mexicans are doing such a splendid job of keeping our food traditions flourishing.

1 Red and Green

Every state in the country boasts an official state song, bird, tree, and flower. New Mexico also lays claim to other symbols, including chiles and frijoles as our official vegetables and the legislatively approved state question of "red or green?" The question refers to chiles, of course, and is heard constantly in restaurants when servers need to know a guest's preference for a particular dish. They are actually the same pod, picked green before maturity and red when ripe. If the diner wants both types, New Mexicans often simply say, "Christmas."

Probably no food in any other state—not lobsters in Maine, pork in Iowa, nor beef in Texas—ranks as highly in the culture as chiles do in New Mexico. They season most New Mexican dishes in one way or another, defining the essence of our traditional cooking, and they also are a major crop economically, a top export, and for many New Mexicans, a virtual addiction. When an out-of-state native New Mexican feels homesick, they almost always yearn for their family and chile, not necessarily in that order.

The world's first chiles probably grew wild as tiny berries in the jungles of present-day Bolivia and Peru at least nine thousand years ago. Migrating birds, possibly aided by human traders, carried the seeds north to central Mexico. The Aztecs called the pungent fruit *chiltepin*, which meant "flea chile" in their language, and they revered its potency. Over time plant breeders in the fertile region transformed the petite berry into the species *Capsicum annuum* and developed a variety of individual cultivars such as the jalapeño and the poblano. When the Spanish came to New Mexico to settle, they brought this species with them to the Santa Fe area, where chile crops thrived in the high-desert climate.

During the next two centuries, before the rest of the country knew anything about chiles, the fiery fruit became the distinguishing feature of New Mexican cooking. Lacking a local source for most other spices and seasonings, cooks literally developed traditional dishes around the flavor of chile. Then as now, it wasn't added to food as a finishing touch, like most sauces, but was a core component of a meal. You ate chile almost daily, or you didn't eat at all.

After the United States seized and occupied New Mexico, settlers moved into the southern part of the territory along the valley of the Rio Grande, destined to become the future center of chile cultivation in the nation. Here, in the budding town of Las Cruces, in 1889 the territorial government established the New Mexico College of Agriculture and Mechanic Arts. The school hired one of the five students in its initial graduating class, Fabian Garcia, as a crop research specialist for its Agricultural Experiment Station. In this position he became the first of an impressive succession of chile experts who bred the plant to produce a singular New Mexico variety of *Capsicum annuum*.

Garcia's contribution was "New Mexico No. 9," a longer, milder, and more prolific cultivar than existing local chiles. After Garcia's retirement from a half century of research, in 1950 Roy Harper introduced "New Mexico No. 6," an even milder and higher-yielding version suitable for canning. Harper also started development of a descendant known as "New Mexico 6-4," which was perfected by another breeder, Roy Nakayama. Widely known in his later career as "Mr. Chile," Nakayama gained fame primarily from his "NuMex Big Jim," a hefty, medium-hot variety ideal for making chile rellenos. The current international chile authority Paul Bosland stepped in as the new leader of the New Mexico State University Chile Pepper Breeding and Genetics Program in 1986. In recognition of his innovations and dedication to the job, colleagues call him the "Chileman."

Most of the chiles bred in Las Cruces stayed in the southern part of the state, where the growing season is considerably longer than in the north. Nakayama created the hot, fast-maturing "Española Improved" for northern farmers, but many of the growers continued to rely primarily on local descendants of the original chiles brought by the Spanish. Horticulturists refer to these heirloom lines as "landraces," and they tend to be closely identified with specific geographic areas. They often go by the name of the town where they evolved, such as Chimayó, Dixon, and Velarde chiles. Unlike the commercially refined pods of the south, these varieties have thin, wrinkly skin, little consistency in characteristics, and the distinct flavor of their soil.

In both areas of the state, New Mexico chiles vary substantially in heat and other qualities. Bosland and his cohorts can crank the potential pungency up or down for a particular cultivar, but up to 76 percent of the actual intensity depends on growing conditions. Environmental stress increases tanginess, so climate, rain, temperatures, soil composition, and other considerations matter in significant respects. New Mexico chiles raised outside the state taste different than the same pods harvested near the Rio Grande. Seed from Garcia's "New Mexico # 9" made it to California in the early twentieth century, prospered in the crop-friendly environment, and became known as the "Anaheim," which is less robust in heat and other flavor factors than chiles grown from the same seeds in the higher-stress conditions of New Mexico.

In cooking authentic New Mexican food, it's important to use chiles evolved or developed in the state because they bring out the best in local dishes. Almost equally key for a proper flavor match, whenever possible a cook should seek out chiles grown in New Mexico (see "New Mexico Culinary Resources," page 187). Merely paying attention to these two simple principles gets you a long way toward a vibrant New Mexico feast.

Chile Caribe

The term "chile caribe" can refer to red chile in several different forms, but in this case we're talking about a concentrated chile paste made from dried whole New Mexico pods. Almost all New Mexico cooks in earlier generations and still quite a few today make it ahead to have on hand as the base for red chile sauces, carne adovada, chile con carne, and other dishes. In the past they would mash the chile through a strainer or colander and remove the skin, but most people don't bother with that today. Some caribe makers will swear that you should start with one of the heirloom chiles of the north, such as Chimayó or Española chiles, but given their scarcity we don't push the point. Instead, we emphasize working from whole pods from anywhere in the state rather than ground chile, which tends to lose its aroma and flavor sitting on a shelf. The "caribe" in the name, according to esteemed historian Estevan Arellano, means something wild and powerful, referring originally to the Carib Indians whom the Spanish encountered in the West Indies.

Makes approximately 3 cups

8 ounces (about 20 to 25) dried whole red chile pods, mild, medium hot, or a combination

water

1 teaspoon salt, or to taste

1. Break off the stems and discard the seeds from chile pods (wear rubber or plastic gloves if your skin is sensitive). Cover chile with water in a medium saucepan. Bring it to a quick boil and remove from heat. Let chiles soak in the water until soft, generally about 20 minutes. Taste the soaking water. If bitter, drain off and discard. If not, reserve 2 cups of the liquid.

2. Transfer chiles to a blender. Pour in the reserved 2 cups of soaking water, or 2 cups of fresh water, add salt and puree.

3. If you wish, scrape the chile paste into a strainer and push the mixture through, discarding the bits of skin left behind. Otherwise, chile caribe is ready to be used in red chile recipes or as a flavoring for any dish that begs for a little zip.

Working ahead: Chile caribe will keep for a week refrigerated. Alternatively, it can be frozen for several months. Freezing in ½-cup or 1-cup portions may be best if you don't anticipate using it all at once.

Variations: Some people simmer the mixture a bit before storing it. Others add garlic or other seasonings to the paste, but we prefer to hold those for the dish to be flavored by the caribe.

The Sweet Smell of New Mexico

Nothing says New Mexico better than chiles roasting in the fall over flames in a revolving wire-cage barrel. It's a colorful sight visually and viscerally whether the chiles are red or green, and the aroma arouses taste buds that have been playing wallflowers for years. It's so iconic you now find it happening at grocery stores all over the Southwest and even in some remoter areas of the country.

Everyone who shops at the farmers' markets in Los Alamos and Santa Fe develops at least a nodding acquaintance with Dixon farmer Matt Romero, a natural-born showman in front of a roasting barrel. The roasting requires skill and attention—not to mention serious gloves—for any kind of chile but particularly the small, curly heirloom pods from Dixon. Matt takes full responsibility for spinning the barrel, keeping his assistants busy with sales. Even when out-of-state stores do parking-lot roasts of the easier-to-handle, uniform green chiles of the Hatch region, the New Mexico Department of Agriculture sends out experts and training DVDs to demonstrate the process.

Red Chile Sauce from Whole Pods

When New Mexicans talk about "red chile" or simply "red," they generally mean the sauce that forms a constituent part of a dish. Cooks make the sauce from either dried whole pods, as is the case here, or from ground chile, as in the recipe after this. Like with chile caribe, starting from whole pods not only helps to ensure freshness but also gains a further advantage in fragrance and flavor from the toasting of the dried chile. Use the sauce in enchiladas, burritos, tamales, or other dishes.

Makes approximately 4 cups

8 ounces (about 20 to 25) dried whole red New Mexican chile pods, mild, medium, hot, or a combination

4 cups water or chicken stock (divided use)

2 tablespoons vegetable oil

1 medium onion, minced

3 garlic cloves, minced

1 to 2 teaspoons crumbled dried Mexican oregano or marjoram

1 teaspoon salt, or more to taste

1. Toast dried whole chile pods in a heavy skillet over medium heat until they are warm and release their fragrance, 1 to 2 minutes per side. Remove the chiles from the skillet immediately. When cool enough to handle, break each chile pod into several pieces (wear rubber or plastic gloves if your skin is sensitive), discarding the stem and seeds. Place the chile pieces in a blender and pour in 2 cups of the water or stock. Puree until mostly smooth but with a few flecks of chile still visible in the liquid.

2. Warm the oil in a large saucepan over medium heat. Add the onion and garlic, and sauté several minutes until the onion is limp. Pour in the blended chile mixture, then add oregano (or marjoram) and salt. Stir the remaining 2 cups of water or stock into the sauce. Reduce the heat to medium low and simmer for a total of 20 to 25 minutes. After about 15 minutes, taste the sauce and adjust seasonings. When ready, the sauce will be cooked down enough to coat a spoon thickly but still drop off of it easily. Use warm or refrigerate for later use.

Working ahead: The sauce keeps for 5 to 6 days refrigerated and freezes well.

Variations: In some cases, cooks will stretch the sauce by adding flour or cornstarch as a thickener, but it's really unnecessary and when overdone is completely undesirable. Some cooks would say to leave out the onion, thinking it distracts from the star ingredient. Early Anglo settlers sometimes tried to tamp down the piquancy of red chile with the addition of tomato, but that's pretty much recognized as heresy today, even by newcomers.

Red Chile Sauce from Ground Pods

Ground dried chile has some pluses for making sauce if you're sure it's freshly ground. It simplifies the process and also facilitates the blending of various chiles with different degrees of heat, earthiness, sweetness, or other characteristics to make a signature sauce for a special dish. In New Mexico it's fairly easy to find superb ground chile at farmers' markets, specialty shops, or grocery stores with high turnover, but the search may be more problematic out of state. Smell it if you can, or at least verify that it's a vibrant crimson red in color.

Makes approximately 4 cups

2 tablespoons vegetable oil

1 medium onion, minced

3 garlic cloves, minced

¾ cup ground dried red chile, mild, medium, hot, or a combination

4 cups chicken or beef stock, or water

1 teaspoon crumbled dried Mexican oregano or marjoram

1 teaspoon salt, or more to taste

1. Warm the oil in a heavy saucepan over medium heat. Add the onion and garlic, and sauté until the onion is limp. Stir in the chile and then the stock or water a cup at a time. Add the oregano (or marjoram) and salt, and bring the sauce just to a boil. Reduce the heat to a low simmer and cook for about 20 minutes. The completed sauce should coat a spoon thickly but still drop off it easily. Use warm or refrigerate for later use.

Working ahead: The sauce keeps for 5 to 6 days refrigerated, and freezes well.

Variations: The onion may be left out. Very occasionally you might find a touch of cumin in red chile, but that's considered Texas falderal in many quarters.

Eat to Live and Live to Eat

Most of us eat for pleasure and some eat for health. You do both when you enjoy the selected Spanish dishes prepared from the recipes in this cookbook. To the uninitiated, some of these foods may seem rather highly seasoned with chile pepper, which gives them their distinctive and delightful flavor. But once you try them, you will like them— and chile is one of the most healthful foods you can eat.

—ELOISA DELGADO DE STEWART, *EL PLATO SABROSO RECIPES* (1941)

September's Simply Chopped Roasted Red

Most red chiles are dried as soon as they are picked, but they also taste delicious freshly roasted like a green pod if you find them at a farmers' market or grow them yourself. They can be substituted in any preparation calling for green chiles, but like red bell peppers they will be sweeter than less mature fruits. We prefer them alone, simply chopped and salted. Though we seldom use garlic salt, it works well with the sweet juices of red chiles as long as it hasn't gone stale in the bottle.

Serves 4

4 to 12 meaty roasted, peeled mild to medium-hot fresh red New Mexican chiles (see How to Roast Fresh Chiles at Home, at left, and How to Steam and Peel Fresh Chiles, page 26)

salt or freshly purchased garlic salt

4 or more warm flour tortillas

1. Chop chiles roughly and add salt to taste. The mixture can be warmed, but it's just fine eaten at room temperature.

2. Serve mounded on a communal plate or in a bowl, accompanied by tortillas. Tear off pieces of tortilla and eat along with bites of the heavenly red.

Working ahead: The chopped chiles can be kept refrigerated for a couple of days but the flavor begins to fade after that. After removing from the fridge, let them sit at room temperature for 30 minutes or so before serving. The chile can be warmed if you wish.

TIP

How to Roast Fresh Chiles at Home

It's easy in an oven, on top of a gas stove, or on an outdoor grill. Let's start with green chiles, the ones most frequently roasted. Plan on 20 minutes for oven roasting, putting the green chiles in a single layer on a baking sheet and blistering them at 450° F until the skins have blackened in many spots. Turn as needed for uniform scorching until the chiles look collapsed. If you are only roasting a couple of pods, hold them with tongs over the flame of a gas burner for a few minutes, turning to blacken all over, or use an asador, a wire-mesh griddle available from "New Mexico Culinary Resources" (page 187). Place the green chiles on the grate over a hot fire on a gas or charcoal grill, searing them on all sides for about 10 minutes. Roast fresh red pods the same ways, but their higher moisture content will keep them from blistering and blackening as fully. To judge readiness, look for loosening skin and a deep brown shade.

Green Chile Sauce

In the days before freezers, and before southern New Mexico growers focused fully on the potential of harvesting chiles green, green sauces were far less common than red. The immature chile turned red in the field rather quickly, making the green pod highly seasonal. Now New Mexico may be more green than red. We prefer to use stock in place of water in both kinds of sauces but especially with green chile for the meatier flavor that used to come from lard or beef suet as the only available cooking fats.

Makes approximately 4 cups

2 tablespoons vegetable oil

½ to 1 medium onion, chopped fine

2 to 3 garlic cloves, minced

1 tablespoon all-purpose flour

2 cups chopped roasted mild to medium-hot New Mexico green chile, fresh or thawed frozen

2 cups chicken or beef stock

½ teaspoon salt, or more to taste

1. Warm the oil in a heavy saucepan over medium heat. Add the onion and garlic and sauté until the onion is soft and translucent, about 5 minutes.

2. Stir in the flour and continue cooking for another 1 or 2 minutes. Mix in the chile. Immediately begin pouring in the stock, stirring as you go, then add the salt. Bring the mixture to a boil. Reduce the heat to a low simmer and cook for about 15 minutes, until thickened but still very pourable. Use warm or refrigerate for later use.

Working ahead: The sauce keeps for about 3 days refrigerated or freezes well.

Variations: Cooks desiring a still meatier sauce may want to brown off a bit of ground or cubed pork loin or beef chuck with the onion and garlic mixture and then simmer the sauce longer, until the meat is tender.

TIP
How to Steam and Peel Fresh Chiles

After roasting chiles, steam them immediately to loosen the skins. Place pods in a Ziplock plastic bag or a covered bowl and let them sit five to ten minutes or until cool enough to handle. If dealing with any quantity of chiles, wear rubber gloves to avoid getting capsaicin (the substance that gives the pods heat) on your hands; it doesn't wash off easily and can irritate the skin. Strip off the peel. You may find yourself wanting to run water over the chiles to help with the process since some peel is bound to stick. Don't do it any more than absolutely necessary, however, because it dilutes flavor. Instead, rinse your gloved hands under the running water. Remove stems and seeds unless you are planning to stuff the chiles, in which case it's better to leave the stem and any seeds still attached to avoid weakening the pod.

Chile Verde Table Relish

Before green chile sauces surged in popularity, cooks often made the green pod into this kind of table seasoning, to be spooned from a bowl over beans, tortillas, meat, or almost anything else. Garlic salt or powder has been a widespread chile flavoring for decades, but we prefer to use a fresh clove to rub the chile container, following the lead of Fabiola Cabeza de Baca Gilbert in *The Good Life: New Mexico Traditions and Food.* This seminal book, published in 1949, didn't even include a recipe for the green chile sauce so familiar now.

Makes about 1 cup

1 garlic clove, halved

6 to 8 meaty roasted peeled mild to hot New Mexico green chiles, fresh or thawed frozen, at room temperature

salt

splash or 2 of cider or white vinegar, optional

splash or 2 of vegetable oil, optional

1. Rub a small bowl with both sides of the garlic clove. Rub until the clove begins to disintegrate, then discard it.

2. Chop chiles roughly and stir in the bowl with salt to taste. If you like the notion, stir in a little oil and vinegar. The amount should be minimal, just enough to coat the chiles rather than turn the relish into a vinaigrette. Serve at room temperature.

Enticing Fruit

Some crops lure a person, or a people, into projecting their desires and hopes upon them, and gradually they yield to the human imperative to become what is desired. Difficult, stubborn, attractive, fiery, chile is one of those, perhaps the best of all.

—STANLEY CRAWFORD, FROM THE FOREWORD TO *THE CHILE CHRONICLES: TALES OF A NEW MEXICO HARVEST* (1997)

Traditional Dried Green Chile

Before refrigeration and freezing, farmers and gardeners dried chiles and other fruits and vegetables to preserve them through the winter. A peeled and dried green chile is still sometimes referred to as chile *pasado*, signifying something from the past. Many families used a clothesline for the drying, as Los Alamos scientist Vic Hogsett remembers his mother and grandmother doing in the San Francisco River valley of Catron County. The process requires several warm, dry, and mostly sunny days, along with a framed screen (like a freshly washed window screen) and some cheesecloth. Reconstitute the chiles as needed by soaking them in warm water for about 30 minutes, then treat them as you would fresh or thawed frozen green chile.

Makes whatever quantity you desire

fresh roasted, peeled whole New
   Mexican green chile pods (see
   How to Roast Fresh Chiles at
   Home, page 25, and How to
   Steam and Peel Fresh Chiles,
   page 26)

1. Lay the chiles on a screen in a single layer, leaving space for air to circulate between the pods. Place the screen in a spot that will be lightly shaded all day (direct sunlight will zap their color). Cover with a single layer of cheesecloth stretched lightly, to keep flies and other insects away from the pods. It's best to bring the chile-strewn screen in at night to avoid critters nosing around it. (Also, bring the screen inside if rain threatens.)

2. Return the screen to the outdoors the next morning. Turn chiles once daily to dry evenly. In most areas of New Mexico, the chiles will dry in 3 to 4 days.

3. Once completely dry, store in glass jars or Ziplock plastic bags.

Working ahead: The whole point of drying the chiles is for storage. They can be kept for up to a year.

A plaque from the Chile Pepper Institute bestows the honorific "First Lady" title on Emma Jean Cervantes. She has hung the gift proudly in her office, facing the desk, though she needs no reminders today about her stature in the world of chile.

It was different early on. Emma Jean met a lot of resistance from men in the initial years of her career as a farmer and entrepreneur in the Mesilla Valley. Time and again she overcame the bias against women engaged in "men's work" and shattered one glass ceiling after another. She and her three children took the family's agricultural business into chile growing and processing, relying on Emma Jean's insight about adding value to the crop through the production of mash for hot-sauce manufacturers. Cervantes Enterprises is now the largest chile processor in New Mexico, handling up to fifty million pounds of pods per year.

On top of all this Emma Jean is also a passionate home cook. She makes her own flour tortillas and sopaipillas, and loves cooking and eating New Mexican favorites such as chile con carne, carne adovada, pork tamales, and quince empanaditas.

2 Breakfast Specialties

It's possible, if such a thing could be measured, that New Mexicans like a hearty breakfast as much or even more than Americans from other states. A substantial percentage of our most popular restaurants specialize in the meal, and they offer a broad variety of robust morning dishes virtually unknown beyond our borders. New Mexicans may not cook a big breakfast at home most of the time, but when we have a chance to jump-start the day properly we relish a good feed.

The allure may go back to the early years of Spanish settlement, when people with sufficient leisure often enjoyed two breakfasts. The first, shortly after awakening, was always light, but the second was much more ample. In her 1846 journal about traveling in New Mexico, Susan Shelby Magoffin described a typical day of meals in the home of friends. "We take coffee about 7½ o'clock, breakfast at 10, and dinner at 5—with fruit between meals. Our dishes are all Mexican, but good ones, some are delightful. . . . The courses for dinner are four, one dish at a time; for breakfast two, ending always with beans. Brandy and wine are regularly put on at each meal."

Few New Mexicans sip brandy at breakfast anymore, but we still eat beans along with good helpings of eggs, meat, cheese, tortillas, and potatoes. Each of these staples, alone or together, often comes loaded with chile, making it a fine way to get fired up for the day.

Torta de Huevo Tradicional

One of the earliest documented egg dishes in New Mexico, featured in a variety of historic cookbooks, these crispy fritters epitomize the sunny harmony between eggs and chile. Egg preparations that rose to prominence later, including several that follow, carried the flavor link further, but the natural compatibility between the ingredients shines in basic simplicity here. The torta de huevo may have originated as a meatless meal for religious observances such as Lent, but we love them for breakfast or supper any time of the year.

Serves 2 or more

3 large eggs	pinch or 2 of salt
2 tablespoons all-purpose flour	vegetable oil, for frying
scant ¼ teaspoon baking powder	red chile sauce (page 23 or 24)

1. Separate the eggs, dropping the whites into a medium-size glass or ceramic mixing bowl and placing the yolks in a small bowl. Whisk the yolks with a fork until they lighten a shade and are well combined. Stir into the yolks the flour, baking powder, and salt.

2. Beat the egg whites with an electric mixer on high speed until they hold soft peaks. Gently fold the egg-yolk mixture into the egg whites.

3. Layer several thicknesses of paper towels near the stove. Pour 1 inch of oil into a broad skillet and heat the oil to 375° F.

4. Scoop up a rounded tablespoonful of the batter and ease it into the oil. Within seconds the batter will puff up to 1½ or 2 times its original size. Fry until deep golden brown and crisp, turning as needed to cook evenly. Remove with a slotted spoon and drain on the paper towels. Make a tiny knife cut into the torta to make sure it is firm but not dry at its center. Adjust the oil temperature a bit up or down as needed to fry the rest of the batter. Once you get the hang of the technique, you can cook several at a time as long as they are not crowded in the pan.

5. Ladle warm chile sauce on a platter and top with the tortas. Serve immediately.

Variations: Around the time of statehood, and for decades before and after, many New Mexican cooks liked to add another dimension to this dish with dried shrimp. Associated today with cuisines in Southeast Asia and Africa, the sun-dried shrimp would be pounded and added as a briny flavoring that worked especially well in simple egg preparations. Look for dried-shrimp powder in Asian or other ethnic groceries. Stir in up to 1 teaspoon of the powder in step 1 (leaving out the salt) when adding the flour and baking powder to the egg yolks.

Huevos Rancheros

These might be better named huevos nuevo mexicanos because they are distinctively different from the huevos rancheros enjoyed in Mexico and other parts of the Southwest. Throughout New Mexico, cooks replace the typical tomato-based ranchero sauce with a stouter red or green chile sauce. Try a "Christmas" mixture of the chiles, with red on one egg and green on the other, and if you have any leftover chile con carne or carne adovada in the fridge they make a great side with this or any other egg dish. Accompany with pinto or refried beans.

Serves 4

vegetable oil for frying

8 corn tortillas (see variation, page 137)

8 large eggs

about 2 tablespoons unsalted butter or bacon drippings

salt

freshly milled black pepper

about 2 cups red or green chile sauce (pages 23 or 24 and 26), or 1 cup of each, warmed

4 ounces (about ½ cup) shredded mild cheddar, Monterey Jack, or asadero cheese

1. Heat about ¼ inch of oil in a medium to large skillet. Dip the tortillas into the oil, 1 or 2 at a time, and cook for a few seconds until soft and pliable. Drain the tortillas and arrange 2 overlapping on each of 4 plates.

2. Break the eggs, 2 by 2, into cups or small bowls.

3. Pour out of the skillet all but enough oil to generously coat the surface. Warm the skillet again over medium heat for 1 to 2 minutes. Add 1 to 2 teaspoons of butter (or bacon drippings), and when the foam subsides, in about 1 minute, pour in the eggs and begin to fry them, 2 to 4 at a time, depending on the skillet size. Cook for 1 minute, seasoning generously with salt and freshly milled black pepper while the eggs cook. As they cook, use a spatula to scoop up some of the butter to drizzle over the whites. Then turn the heat down to low and continue cooking and drizzling the butter for about 1 additional minute, or until done to your liking. Repeat with the remaining eggs, adding more butter to the skillet as necessary.

4. Top each tortilla with a fried egg. Ladle chile sauce over and around the eggs. If using both red and green sauces, pour 1 over 1 egg on each plate, and the second over the other. Sprinkle with cheese. Serve the eggs immediately.

Springing Awake

I think New Mexico was the greatest experience from the outside world that I have ever had. It certainly changed me for ever. Curious as it may sound, it was New Mexico that liberated me from the present era of civilization, the great era of material and mechanical development. . . . In the magnificent fierce morning of New Mexico one sprang awake, a new part of the soul woke up suddenly, and the old world gave way to a new.

—D. H. LAWRENCE, *PHOENIX: THE POSTHUMOUS PAPERS* (1936)

Green Chile Cheese Omelet

Lots of New Mexico dishes combine chile, cheese, and eggs, a classic merger of elemental flavors. Some cooks put them together in breakfast burritos or enchiladas, others in chile rellenos casseroles, and others still in baked snack squares. Of all the options, this one may be the best, a popular eye-opener where the three tastes meld beautifully and equally.

Serves 1

2 extra-large or large eggs

salt

freshly milled black pepper

1 tablespoon water or milk

1 tablespoon unsalted butter

3 ounces (about ⅓ cup) shredded mild or sharp cheddar cheese or crumbled mild creamy goat cheese

about ½ cup green chile sauce (page 26), warmed

1. Briefly whisk the eggs together in a bowl with the salt, pepper, and water (or milk). Whisk just enough to combine the yolks and the whites.

2. Warm the butter in a 7- to 8-inch omelet pan or skillet, preferably nonstick, over high heat. Swirl the pan to coat the entire surface thoroughly. Just when the butter begins to color, add the egg mixture and swirl it to coat the entire surface as well. Let the pan sit directly over the heat for a few seconds, until the eggs just begin to set in the bottom of the pan. Scatter half of the cheese over the eggs. Pull the pan sharply toward you several times, and then tilt the pan and use a heatproof rubber spatula to fold the front half of the omelet over the back portion. Tip the omelet out onto a heatproof serving plate, neatening it with the spatula if needed.

3. Pour chile sauce over the omelet and top with the remaining cheese. Serve immediately.

How to Make a Great Omelet

- If you're investing in an omelet pan, buy a nonstick one and a heatproof rubber spatula to go with it.

- Premeasure all the ingredients required for the number of omelets you're making and have them handy.

- If making more than one, mix up each batch of eggs separately for the best results. Just wipe out the pan between omelets. The process goes quickly enough to serve several guests.

- Unlike most other egg preparations, omelets should be cooked over high heat, in a pan that's hot enough to sizzle a drop of water. Remember that the egg will continue to cook off of the heat, so remove the omelet from the stove just before the preferred doneness.

- Fillings should be modest in portions, cut in small pieces. Anything you put inside an omelet should already be at the temperature wanted for serving. The egg surrounding the filling will only provide enough heat for the melting of cheese and not much else.

Variations: The so-called "Spanish omelet" is no more Iberian than Spanish rice. It's a product instead of the American West and has plenty of fans in New Mexico who enjoy it with chile. Tomatoes form the core of the filling and the sauce everywhere, supplemented in New Mexico by sautéed green chile, onion, and maybe a bit of sage, mushrooms, or finely chopped ham. To make a basic version of the filling, warm 1 tablespoon of butter in a small saucepan over medium heat, add 1 tablespoon each of finely chopped onion and minced green chile and cook the mixture for 1 minute. Add salt and 1 cup of chopped fresh or drained canned tomatoes and cook for about 5 minutes, just until the liquid is thick instead of watery. Fill the omelet with about ⅔ of the mixture, saving the rest to spoon over the completed omelet before serving. The Junior League of Albuquerque's 1981 *Simply Simpático* cookbook uses a similar style sauce in Tiered Omelet Rancheros, 4 flat omelets stacked like layers of a cake with the sauce ladled on top. Avocado slices, dollops of sour cream, and shredded Monterey Jack cheese top the dish. The extravaganza is sliced into wedges like a cake to serve.

Grants Quiki

Old Route 66 used to abound with down-home cafés, but many closed when Interstate 40 replaced the original highway and brought in the fast-food joints. The Uranium Café in Grants was an exception for decades, but it too shut the doors in recent years. The café's specialty was the Quiki, an unusual combination of scrambled eggs, canned hominy, and one or more choices of chorizo, ham, green chile, and cheese. Here's our re-creation of it, with our favorite of the additions. A version of this appeared in our book *A Real American Breakfast* (2002).

Serves up to 4

6 large eggs

3 tablespoons whipping cream
   or half-and-half

salt

freshly milled black pepper

¼ pound bulk chorizo or other
   spicy bulk sausage

up to 2 tablespoons unsalted
   butter

14½- to 15½-ounce can of
   hominy, preferably yellow,
   drained

1. Briefly whisk together the eggs in a bowl with cream, salt, and pepper. Combine only long enough for the mixture to become uniformly yellow, with large bubbles still evident.

2. Fry the chorizo in a large heavy skillet over medium heat until well browned and cooked through. Break the chorizo into small pieces with a spatula as it cooks. You will want about 2 tablespoons of fat to cook the eggs. Add as much of the butter to the skillet as needed. When the butter is melted, add the hominy and heat through. Scoop out about ½ cup of the hominy–chorizo mixture and reserve it. Reduce the heat to medium low.

3. Pour the eggs into the skillet. Cook, stirring frequently from the bottom with a spatula until the eggs form soft curds and are lightly set but still look a little runny, 3 to 4 minutes. Do not overcook. Remove from the heat, and stir an additional time or two to cook through. Divide among plates and top each portion with a couple of tablespoons of the reserved hominy. Serve immediately.

La Hacienda de los Martinez

Maybe the most fascinating *casa mayor* (great house) surviving in the Southwest, Hacienda de los Martinez in Taos provides an authentic glimpse into nineteenth-century Hispano life and culture in New Mexico. A fortresslike structure with massive adobe walls, it was built in 1804 as the residence of Severino and Maria del Carmel Santistevan Martinez but also served as a regional trade center and the headquarters of a large ranching and farming operation. The eldest son of the family, Padre Antonio Martinez, became a famous defender of local Catholic practices in conflicts he had with the French Archbishop Lamy.

In the hacienda's heyday, much of daily life took place outside in two inner courtyards, where servants cooked and baked, processed wool, and did most of the home and farm chores. At night and during bad weather, everyone went to one of the twenty-one rooms inside. Visitors interested in food will be intrigued in particular by the *dispensa*, essentially a large refrigerator that maintained a constant cool temperature; the *granero* that holds three big bins for storing wheat, corn, and barley; and the *cocina*, which has a remarkable "shepherd's fireplace" capable of cooking meals for dozens of people at a time.

Smothered Breakfast Burritos

In a state where enchiladas are a common breakfast dish, often topped with a fried egg, the idea of a morning burrito is a no-brainer. Locals have probably eaten them informally for many years, filling a flour tortilla with leftover beans or meat or even freshly fried bacon to eat on the run. More elaborate, plated versions smothered in chile, now ubiquitous in restaurants, developed more recently, perhaps no earlier than 1975 when Tia Sophia's opened in downtown Santa Fe. Certainly the bustling café created a premier rendition and played a substantial role in putting the dish on the culinary map. This burrito, modeled on theirs, shouts "Good Morning!" with an emphatically New Mexican accent.

Serves 4 generously

¼ cup vegetable oil

3 large russet potatoes, peeled or unpeeled, shredded on the large holes of a box grater or in a food processor

½ teaspoon salt

freshly ground black pepper

1 medium onion, chopped

1 garlic clove, minced

2 large eggs, lightly beaten, optional

4 flour tortillas, warmed

8 slices bacon, cooked until crisp

3 to 4 cups green chile sauce (page 26), warmed

6 to 8 ounces mild cheddar cheese, shredded

1. Preheat the oven to 400° F.

2. Warm the oil in a large heavy skillet over medium heat. Stir in the potatoes, salt, and as much pepper as you wish. Pat the mixture down evenly and cook several minutes. Scrape it up from the bottom of the skillet, add the onion and garlic, and pat back down again. Repeat the process until the potatoes are cooked through and golden brown, with many crisp edges, about 12 to 15 minutes. If you are including eggs, pour them over the potatoes and scrape the mixture up and down another couple of times to distribute and cook the eggs.

3. Spoon ¼ of the potatoes onto a tortilla. Top it with 2 slices of bacon. Roll up into a loose cylinder and place the burrito seam-side down on a heatproof plate. Spoon ¼ of the chile sauce over the burrito and sprinkle it generously with cheese. Repeat with the remaining ingredients.

4. Bake the burritos until the cheese is melted and gooey, about 5 minutes. Serve immediately.

Variations: Chicharrones, carnitas, beans, sausage, salsa, and bits of crunchy corn tortillas are just a few of the other ingredients that can be stuffed into a morning burrito. Use your imagination and follow your taste buds in the manner of Consuelo Flores, the Burrito Lady of Albuquerque's Northeast Heights, who offers about a dozen different breakfast burrito combinations daily from her small storefront.

No Flakes Here

Breakfast turned out to be the meal I always had on my own while I was in Santa Fe. I could picture Nan nibbling on some yogurt and fresh fruit as she contemplated what our lunch and dinner were going to be like, but I tried not to let that spoil my appetite. In fact, one morning, as I began thinking about how few mealtimes there were before my departure compared to how many chile-pits I had left to visit, I downed back-to-back breakfast burritos—first at a place near the Plaza called Tia Sophia's and then at Horseman's Haven, a café that occupies part of an abandoned filling station. . . . In both places, I had half of the burrito covered in green chile and the other half covered in red—a combination that people in Santa Fe sometimes call Christmas. It beats cornflakes by a mile.

—CALVIN TRILLIN, "BOWLFUL OF DREAMS," *GOURMET* (OCTOBER 2002)

Papas Fritas Suprema

Fried potatoes. What better way to kick off the day in a hearty fashion? Leftover baked or boiled potatoes can be cooked up pretty quickly, but when you have a leisurely weekend morning, or want breakfast for Sunday-night supper, try this technique. These fried potatoes will take about an hour to prepare, though they don't require much attention. Starting with raw potato cubes allows them to develop the ultimate in contrast between crunchy exteriors and creamy insides.

Serves 4

2 tablespoons bacon drippings or lard, or unsalted butter or vegetable oil

1¾ pounds (about 3 medium) russet or Yukon Gold potatoes, peeled and cut in ¾-inch cubes

½ teaspoon salt, or more to taste

freshly milled black pepper

½ medium onion, diced

shredded Monterey Jack or asadero cheese, optional

red or green chile sauce (pages 23 or 24 and 26), warmed

1. Warm the drippings in a 10- to 12-inch cast-iron skillet over medium-low heat. Stir in the potatoes, and when coated with fat season them with ½ teaspoon salt and several grindings of pepper. Cover the skillet and cook for 20 minutes, during which time you should hear only a faint cooking sound.

2. Uncover the potatoes and fry for approximately 30 minutes longer. After the first 10 minutes, scatter the onions over the potatoes, and scrape the mixture back up, turning the potatoes over, and pat back down. After 10 more minutes, scrape up, turn, and pat down again. As the potatoes soften, pat them down more lightly, but bring as much of their surface in contact with the skillet as possible without mashing them. In the last 10 minutes or so of cooking, bring the heat up to medium and turn the potatoes at 5-minute intervals. Add more salt and pepper if you wish. The papas are ready when the potato cubes are richly browned with crisp surfaces and tender, melting centers.

3. Plate them up immediately, scatter with optional cheese, and ladle chile sauce over and around. Serve piping hot.

Variations: Yukon Golds or another medium-starch potato can be substituted for the higher-starch russets. If chile sauce doesn't appeal as a topping, you might want to add a little color with about half of a bell pepper, diced. Add it with the onion. Papas, or papitas, are considered something of an art form in breakfast restaurants, and mountainous piles of potatoes are offered with eggs, chile con carne, carne adovada, carnitas, gravy, vegetable sautés, and other additions beyond just chile sauce and cheese.

Candido Valerio grew up just northwest of Ranchos de Taos in the tiny community of Los Cordovas. Born in the early 1920s, he has seen sweeping cultural changes in New Mexico during the twentieth century and beyond. His family, like others of the village, used to produce pretty much everything they needed. When the Great Depression came, he recalls, "Money was pretty much unknown to us. If you don't have it, you don't miss it. We never went to a store. We raised what we needed or exchanged something with our neighbors to get it."

His family grew white corn among many other crops. Some of the corn was harvested young, or "green," and the ears still in their husks went into a heated and sealed outdoor horno oven, where they smoldered overnight. Some of the corn was saved for chicos (page 130), but part of it was taken to the community water mill run by his uncle. There it would be ground into flour with the water that flowed through the local acequia. His family used the toasted corn flour to make their *chaquehue*, which they ate most mornings.

Candido says, "It was the best 'oatmeal' ever." He remembers it as a telling feature of "a very good life" of self-sufficiency before the days of money and stores.

A Bowl of Blue

Called *chaquewa* or *chaquehue*, or sometimes atole (a name usually reserved for a similar beverage), blue-corn porridge in some form dates back centuries as a nourishing New Mexican meal. It remains particularly popular today in the pueblos, where it is most often a breakfast dish. Folks who didn't grow up with it, and even some who did, like it best with the addition of some kind of sweetener, and perhaps some raisins, nuts, or a splash of warm milk. Anyone who enjoys oatmeal or other warm cereals should give this a try. If cooking just for yourself or for two, it's easy to reduce the recipe proportionately.

Serves 4

4 cups water	sugar, brown sugar, or agave nectar
2 cups fine-ground blue cornmeal	raisins, pecans, or piñon nuts
¾ teaspoon salt	warm milk, optional

1. Bring water in a large saucepan to a boil over high heat. Pour cornmeal in slowly, stirring as you go. When the cornmeal is incorporated, add salt and turn the heat down until just an occasional bubble breaks around the edges. Stir regularly until thickened into a cream-of-wheat-like porridge, about 10 minutes.

2. Spoon into bowls and offer sugar and other mix-ins on the side. Eat right away.

Requesón

Back at the time of statehood, many New Mexicans made their own cheese as a way of extending the life of milk from their goats and cows. Liquid rennet, collected from the stomachs of butchered livestock, coagulated the milk and formed curds. The initial cheese would be a creamy thick queso, possibly molded in a section of an old coffee can and similar to fresh goat-milk cheeses found nationwide today. The remaining whey contained enough protein to turn it into a lighter, grainier ricotta-like cheese called *requesón*, or *requesónes*. At breakfast, the cheese was topped with a drizzle of molasses, honey, cane or sorghum syrup, or even jelly. You can make the cheese from your own whey (following any ricotta recipe), buy commercial *requesón* today in some markets, or substitute ricotta mixed with some cottage cheese, and top it with one of the sweeteners. Berries or other soft-textured summer fruit are also a nice extra.

Serves 4

2 cups *requesón* or 1½ cups ricotta cheese and ½ cup drained small-curd cottage cheese

molasses, honey, cane syrup, sorghum syrup, or agave nectar

1. If you are combining ricotta and cottage cheese, mash the cottage cheese with a fork and then mix in the ricotta.

2. Spoon cheese into bowls. Accompany with your choice of sweet syrups.

Variations: Some cooks stir in a greater portion of cottage cheese to get the texture they consider most truly New Mexican. Start with the substitution of ½ cup and work up from there if you wish up to a half-and-half mixture of each. Granola or trail mix makes a good topping, too. The cheese makes a nice accompaniment to Pumpkin Piñon Bread (page 148).

Making New Mexico Molasses

Don Teodoro and José ate their breakfast by lamplight while Tilano hitched the horses to the wagon which was to bring the sugar cane to the press to be ground. Their small subsistence acreage had not allowed them to plant much cane but there was enough to turn into molasses for the family table. On the day before, Don Teodoro and José had cut the cane with a sickle and now they were bringing it to the yard of their house where the cane mill stood.

José unhitched the horses from the wagon and hitched one to the pole that controlled the lever which turned the cane mill. Don Teodoro fed the stalks to the rollers which were set on a block and as José drove the horse, the rollers ground the cane and extracted the juice. A trough made from two boards extended from the mill frame and this served to carry the juice into a large kettle. As soon as one container filled up, Tilano took it to Doña Paula who was waiting to strain it into the copper kettle which was used for making the molasses.

—FABIOLA CABEZA DE BACA GILBERT, *THE GOOD LIFE: NEW MEXICO TRADITIONS AND FOOD* (1949)

Many towns around the world celebrate a special pancake day, usually on Shrove Tuesday, the day before the beginning of Lent on Ash Wednesday. The tradition in England goes back to the medieval period, when pancakes represented a feast of sugar, fat, and eggs, foods usually restricted during Lent. The custom is analogous to Mardi Gras festivities in other places and continues most famously in the United States in the annual pancake race rivalry between Liberal, Kansas, and Olney, England, that began in 1950.

Santa Fe is in winter hibernation mode at this time of the year, but the residents bring out their pans and cakes in full glory in the summer to welcome the Fourth of July. At the annual Pancakes on the Plaza fiesta, started by Clarence Rumpel, Carl Fisher, and the Chamber of Commerce in 1975, much of the town shows up for a really big breakfast. Some five hundred volunteers staff numerous booths that fry around thirty thousand pancakes of different styles ranging from blue corn piñon to sweet potato pecan varieties. While people nosh for five hours, bands play on the plaza gazebo stage, children compete in a coloring contest, artisans sell their wares, and owners of vintage and cool cars proudly showcase their beloved carriages.

Blue Corn Piñon Pancakes

Many New Mexicans love blue corn pancakes and others pine for piñon pancakes, but for our tastes the two iconic ingredients really bring out the best in each other when combined. You can simply sprinkle piñon nuts into the batter, but grinding some of them imparts their subtle flavor more fully through the fluffy hotcakes.

Serves 4

1¼ cups piñon nuts (divided use)

¾ cup fine- or medium-ground blue cornmeal

½ cup plus 2 tablespoons all-purpose flour

1 tablespoon sugar

¾ teaspoon baking powder

¾ teaspoon salt

2 tablespoons unsalted butter, melted

2 large eggs

1¼ cups milk

2 drops of almond extract

vegetable oil for frying

unsalted butter

maple syrup or sliced fresh apricots or peaches

1. Grind ¾ cup of the nuts in a food processor with the cornmeal, processing by pulsing briefly several times. Stop when a coarse meal forms and before the soft nuts turn to butter. Add the flour, sugar, baking powder, and salt, and pulse several more times, until mixed together, then pour in the butter and pulse until it disappears. Add the eggs, milk, and almond extract and pulse a few more times to combine. Transfer the batter to a mixing bowl, if you wish, or use it from the processor bowl directly. Stir in the remaining nuts.

2. Warm a griddle, preferably, or a large heavy skillet over medium heat. Pour a thin film of oil on the griddle. Pour or spoon out the batter onto the hot griddle, where it should sizzle and hiss. A generous 3 tablespoons of batter will make a 4-inch pancake. Make as many cakes as you can fit on the surface without crowding.

3. Flip the pancakes after 1 to 2 minutes, when their edges begin to look dry and start to brown. The pancakes are done when the second side is golden brown, an additional 1 to 2 minutes. Repeat with the remaining batter, adding a bit more oil to the griddle as needed.

4. Serve the pancakes immediately, with butter and either syrup or fruit.

3 Soups, Salads, and Appetizers

At least by the early nineteenth century, and probably before, dinner in upper-crust New Mexico homes usually began with soup. It was generally a midday meal then, what we now consider lunch, and the soup whetted the appetite for hearty courses to come. The starter was often little more than a tasty broth made by boiling down meat bones and remnants, perhaps with the addition of garden castoffs or dried beans, peas, or corn. On formal or celebratory occasions, more went into the pot, sometimes blurring the line between soup and stew.

In the last half of the twentieth century, salad frequently usurped from soup the dinner debut role. Just as there were seldom real recipes for anything except the most special soups, this became the case for salads, too. Cooks in a hurry simply raided the garden or refrigerator for what was available to toss together, but some situations called for a more structured if still simple approach, as we suggest for a few notable salads.

Other types of starters have been less common in New Mexico, perhaps because traditional main courses tend to be filling and varied on their own. We offer a couple of options, however, dishes that both speak to our culinary heritage and are guaranteed to wake up the taste buds.

Sopa de Albóndigas

With roots that go back to Spain, and clones that have spread across the Americas, this broth with meatballs has been the New Mexican soup of choice for generations, perhaps since the colonial period. Our ancestors didn't tinker as much with this dish as they did with many others, but they sometimes added blue cornmeal, a touch we still like today. Often served at holiday and homecoming meals, albóndigas take center stage in an annual December feast at the Tortugas Pueblo near Las Cruces. As a part of the three-day fiesta honoring Our Lady of Guadalupe, cooks roll enough meatballs to feed about four hundred people who patiently wait their turn in line to sit and enjoy the meal in the pueblo's Casa de la Comida, a community kitchen and dining hall.

Serves 6 to 8

Albóndigas

1 tablespoon olive oil

½ small onion, minced

1 small celery rib, chopped fine

1½ pounds ground lamb, beef, or veal, or a combination

¼ cup plus 2 tablespoons blue cornmeal

1 large egg

1 to 2 teaspoons dried mint

1 teaspoon salt

1 teaspoon New Mexican azafrán (safflower stamens), optional

Broth

2 tablespoons olive oil (divided use)

½ small onion, minced

1 tablespoon all-purpose flour

14- to 15-ounce can diced tomatoes in juice, preferably "fire-roasted"

2 cups beef or chicken stock

2 cups water

1 teaspoon New Mexican azafrán (safflower stamens), optional

salt

fresh mint leaves, optional

For albóndigas

1. Warm 1 tablespoon olive oil in a small skillet over medium heat. Stir in onion and celery and sauté until soft but not brown, about 5 minutes. Set aside to cool.

2. In a medium bowl, mix together the meat, cornmeal, and egg. Scrape the onion and celery mixture into the meat followed by the remaining ingredients and stir together lightly.

3. Form ¾- to 1-inch meatballs, packing the meat together lightly. If the meat mixture is sticking to your hands, rinse your hands regularly with cold water. You should end up with about 48 small meatballs.

Azafrán

New Mexican azafrán, the dried red-orange stamens of the safflower plant, is served traditionally as a substitute for less available and much pricier true saffron. Purchase it from Hispano markets, the Santa Fe School of Cooking (see New Mexico Culinary Resources, page 187), or substitute a pinch of real Spanish saffron or ¼ teaspoon tumeric for each teaspoon.

For broth

1. Warm 1 tablespoon of olive oil in a large heavy saucepan over medium-high heat. Sear the meatballs, in batches that aren't crowded in the pan, until they are nicely brown, turning them frequently but gently. Drain with a slotted spoon and set aside on a platter.

2. Reduce the heat to medium and add 1 tablespoon of olive oil. Stir in the onion and sauté several minutes until translucent, then add the flour and cook for another minute, stirring.

3. Stir in tomatoes and juice, stock, water, optional azafrán, meatballs, and any juices. Bring just to a boil, then reduce the heat to medium low, cover, and cook for 15 to 20 minutes, until the flavors blend and the meatballs are cooked through. Salt to taste.

4. Ladle into broad shallow soup bowls. If you wish, cut mint leaves into very thin ribbons and shower over the bowls. Serve.

Working ahead: The broth can be made up to 2 days ahead by skipping the initial step of browning the meatballs in 1 tablespoon of oil. The meatballs can be formed a day ahead of when you plan to fry them, but arrange them on an oiled baking sheet and refrigerate. They are best fried shortly before you plan to simmer them in the broth.

Calabacitas Soup

Gayther Gonzales of Tesuque, an avid cook and proprietor of North of the Border chile company, developed and shared this recipe. Both sides of his family came from the rural, agricultural area east of Las Vegas, New Mexico. Gayther's grandmothers taught him to love food and its preparation, making meals he stills remembers from seemingly nothing. As he recalls, "I later learned that was called cooking."

Serves 6 or more

3 tablespoons vegetable or olive oil	¾ teaspoon crumbled dried Mexican oregano
1 large onion, chopped (divided use)	¼ teaspoon cumin
4 large garlic cloves, chopped (divided use)	2 to 3 cups chicken stock
2½ cups yellow corn kernels (divided use)	1 cup chopped roasted New Mexican green chile
5 or 6 medium summer squashes, preferably a combination of zucchini and yellow squash, diced	salt
	freshly ground black pepper
	sour cream, optional
2 medium tomatoes, diced	shredded sharp cheddar cheese

1. Warm the oil in a large saucepan over medium heat. Stir in half of the onion, half of the garlic, and 2 cups of corn kernels and cook until the corn is barely tender, 2 or 3 minutes. Add the squash and tomatoes, along with the oregano and cumin, and enough stock to cover them. Cook until the squash is very tender, 20 to 25 additional minutes. Add the green chile and the remaining garlic and onion. Simmer for about 5 minutes, then remove the soup from the heat and cool briefly.

2. Puree the soup in a blender in 2 batches, pouring in a little more stock if necessary, and return it to the saucepan. Stir in the remaining ½ cup of corn, add salt and pepper to taste, and bring the soup to a boil. Reduce the heat and simmer about 10 minutes longer.

3. Ladle the soup into bowls. Add a dollop of sour cream to each if you wish. Sprinkle cheese over the soup and serve.

Gayther Gonzales Explains His Soup

My grandparents on my mother's side had a small farm in the north valley in Albuquerque. They had an apple orchard and grew a vegetable garden. Our visits were always fun and filling. My grandmother taught me how to make applesauce . . . country style with skin on and chunky. I still make it that way, though I store it in the freezer instead of canning.

She also made some of the best calabacitas I ever tasted. She came from Purcell, Oklahoma, and brought with her a recipe for summer squash and sweet corn casserole. With a few adjustments suggested by my grandfather, and a little green chile, she had a signature New Mexico dish. The recipe was passed on to my mother, who, oddly, has never and will not eat squash. I loved it and have always grown squash in my garden. Sometimes, though, when I skipped a day of tending, I would uncover baseball-bat-size zucchinis and beach-ball-looking yellows, which did not make the best calabacitas. I developed this soup to avoid wasting the overgrown specimens, which I peel and de-seed, then simmer nearly to the fall-apart stage and puree. The soup's even better when you start with small market-size squashes.

Green Chile Chicken Soup

In her *Original New Mexico Cookery* (1916), Alice Stevens Tipton gets a little didactic about soup. About them in general, she says, "The primary object of soups is to warm the stomach and start the gastric juices to flowing, as an aid to digestion. Therefore a soup should be hot when served, and more in the nature of a broth or puree than a chowder. . . . Nothing cold should be taken into the stomach immediately after eating soup, not even a drink of cold water, as it tends to harden any grease contained in the soup, and thereby hinders digestion."

In her recipe for bean soup, Tipton insists that New Mexico beans be used. "No others are 'just as good,' for the beans grown in this state have a richness and flavor far superior to the ordinary bean."

Most home soups are still a combination of ingredients on hand. This blend is tasty enough to make an exception, encouraging you to go out and get a good farm-raised chicken as the basis. The Comida Buena deli at the Albuquerque International Sunport deserves credit for promoting this soup, serving steaming bowls of it to a steady line of pilots, flight attendants, TSA workers, and in-the-know travelers.

Serves 6 or more

1 whole chicken, about 3½ pounds	14- to 15-ounce can diced tomatoes in juice, preferably "fire-roasted"
2 garlic cloves, minced	1 large russet potato, peeled and diced
1 teaspoon crumbled dried Mexican oregano or marjoram	3 to 4 medium carrots, chopped
1 teaspoon ground cumin	2 to 3 celery stalks, chopped
1 teaspoon salt, or more to taste	1½ to 2 cups chopped roasted mild to medium New Mexican green chile
¼ teaspoon freshly ground black pepper	
1 large onion, chopped	

1. Place the chicken in a stockpot or large saucepan. Pour in enough water to cover, then add the garlic, oregano (or marjoram), cumin, 1 teaspoon salt, and pepper. Bring to a boil over high heat, then reduce the heat to a simmer and cook for about 1 hour, until the chicken is very tender. With a large sturdy spoon, remove the chicken from the pot and set it aside to cool on a plate. Add the onion, tomatoes and juice, potato, carrots, and celery to the stock and continue to simmer about 20 minutes longer.

2. Let the chicken cool for about 15 minutes then, while still warm, pull into bite-size shreds or chop into neat cubes. Discard the skin and bones.

3. Return the chicken to the broth and add the green chile. Simmer the soup for 15 to 20 minutes, until the vegetables are very tender and the flavors blended. Add more salt, if needed. Ladle into bowls and serve.

Variations: A few squeezes of lime can be nice, as can some chopped fresh cilantro. Either should be added just after the soup comes off the stove. If you like, scatter a small handful of Monterey Jack cheese in the bottom of each bowl before adding the soup or float a cheesy crouton on the top. You can also turn this into a tortilla soup, adding crisp strips of fried or baked corn tortillas or even a few tortilla chips.

Ensalada Santa Cruz

Tender greens were not a routine part of the New Mexico diet in the early days of statehood. In reviewing literature from that era forward, we periodically came across a vegetable salad with warm bacon dressing sometimes just referred to as "Mexican salad." One of the later books where we found it was the *Española Valley Cookbook* (1975) put together as a fund-raiser by the ladies of the Española Hospital Auxiliary. On this occasion, it was named for Santa Cruz, a historic village not far from Española, and was credited to Lydia Corriz.

Serves 6

1 to 1¼ pounds red-ripe cherry tomatoes, halved

3 medium bell peppers, a combination of colors, sliced into very thin ribbons

4 scallions, white and green portions, sliced into thin rounds

4 slices bacon, chopped

vegetable or olive oil

1 tablespoon sugar

1 teaspoon dried ground New Mexican red chile

½ to 1 teaspoon salt

2 tablespoons cider or white vinegar

1. Arrange the tomatoes, bell peppers, and scallions in a large bowl.

2. Fry the bacon in a skillet over medium heat until brown and crisp. Drain the bacon on paper towels. Add enough oil to the bacon fat in the skillet to equal about ⅓ cup. Add sugar, chile, and salt and stir until the sugar dissolves. Remove the skillet from the heat and stir in vinegar, watching out for splatters.

3. Pour the warm dressing over the vegetables and toss lightly. Sprinkle bacon over the salad and serve.

Variations: This kind of vegetable salad might have replaced lettuce versions in the past, but today there's no reason not to enjoy some greens along with it. Opt for sturdy greens, such as ribbons of romaine or a wedge of crisp cold iceberg under the vegetables. Some crumbles of fresh or aged goat cheese make a fine addition, too.

Ensalada de Col

The Spanish spread cabbage throughout Mexico and the Southwest. Many New Mexico restaurant kitchens limit garnishes today to a bland scattering of lettuce and tomatoes, but this salad mixture is an excellent variation, with enough substance to allow it a stand-alone role. La Posta de Mesilla may be the only restaurant in the state still serving it regularly. It deserves a wider audience again.

Serves 4 to 6

¼ cup vegetable oil

2 tablespoons white or cider vinegar

1 teaspoon freshly ground black pepper

¾ teaspoon salt, or more to taste

½ to 1 teaspoon crushed red chile caribe, optional

3 cups shredded green cabbage

½ small red onion, or other mild onion, sliced into thin half-moons (soak in hot water for 10 minutes first for a milder flavor)

1. In a large bowl mix together the oil, vinegar, pepper, salt, and optional chile. When blended, add cabbage and onion and toss until combined. Add more salt if you wish.

2. Refrigerate 30 minutes and serve.

Watercress Salad with Herb Dressing

Though frequently characterized as a desert, New Mexico is blessed with many mountain streams and warm springs. Watercress grows wild near these as well as along acequias, the patchwork of irrigation ditches used to water domesticated crops. Artist Georgia O'Keeffe, who first settled at Ghost Ranch, eventually moved to a breathtaking parcel in the northern village of Abiquiu where it was easier to have a garden and orchard. She loved to grow, cook, and eat produce from her property and was always pleased to have seasonal wild greens such as cress, quelites, and purslane added to the bounty. Her favorite salad dressing, a revolving mixture of finely cut garden herbs, garlic, and good olive oil, topped this and other salads. The dressing also was used as a marinade for the occasional steak she liked to have supplied by the professionally staffed meat counter at Kaune's Neighborhood Market in Santa Fe. Our thanks to Margaret Wood, cook and companion to O'Keeffe in her later life, for sharing her reminiscences and the recipe, which appeared in her book *A Painter's Kitchen* (1997).

Serves 4

Herb dressing

2 tablespoons olive oil

2 tablespoons safflower oil or other high-quality vegetable oil

1 teaspoon lemon juice, or more to taste

¼ teaspoon whole-grain mustard, such as Dijon

1 garlic clove

2 teaspoons fresh herbs such as lovage, tarragon, dill, basil, or parsley, preferably a combination, chopped

salt

freshly ground black pepper

pinch of sugar, optional

Salad

2 large bunches watercress (about 6 ounces)

1 garlic clove, halved

handful of fresh chives

For dressing

1. In a bowl whisk together the oils, lemon juice, and mustard. Squeeze the garlic clove through a garlic press into the liquid. Add the chopped herbs and salt and pepper to taste. Sprinkle in sugar if needed to balance the tang and tartness. Let the dressing stand for at least 30 minutes and up to an hour for fullest flavor.

Assembly

1. Separate the stems of the cress and wash well, swishing around in a couple of changes of cool water. Pat or spin the leaves dry.

2. Rub a wooden salad bowl well with garlic clove, using the cut side of at least half of the clove.

3. Arrange the watercress in a bowl and pour dressing over it. Toss well. Slice chives into 1-inch lengths and scatter over the salad. Serve right away.

Variations: Margaret notes that if the watercress is too spicy it is acceptable to mix in some tender lettuces. Sliced sweet radishes, tomatoes, jícama, or oranges were—and are—also good additions.

Ensalada de Noche Buena

Hispanos in New Mexico and elsewhere know Christmas Eve as *noche buena* (the good night), and in many warm climes in the Americas a celebratory dinner includes this kind of colorful salad, where ingredients are added almost like ornaments on a Christmas tree. In recent decades, after the tropical elements in the salad became widely available in the state, some New Mexico families have adopted the tradition. This version is based on one we learned from friends in Chimayó.

Serves 6

Dressing

juice and zest from 1 lime

3 tablespoons honey

2 tablespoon cider vinegar

2 tablespoons mayonnaise

1 tablespoon vegetable oil

½ teaspoon ground dried New
    Mexican red chile

¼ teaspoon salt

Salad

4 oranges, peeled, sectioned, and
    cut into bite-size pieces

¾ pound jícama, peeled and cut
    in slim matchsticks

2 bananas

¼ cup chopped cilantro

4 red radishes, slivered

¼ cup roasted salted peanuts,
    chopped

seeds of 1 pomegranate

romaine or other lettuce leaves

For dressing

1. In a blender, puree all the dressing ingredients. Refrigerate until ready to use. The dressing can be prepared a day ahead.

Assembly

1. In a medium bowl, toss together the oranges and jícama and refrigerate for at least 45 minutes. Shortly before serving time, peel and slice the bananas. Add the bananas, cilantro, and radishes to the orange and jícama mixture. Toss with the salad dressing.

2. Line a serving bowl or platter with lettuce leaves. Turn the salad mixture out onto the platter. Scatter peanuts and pomegranate seeds over the salad and serve.

The Lady of the Feast, Norma Naranjo

Norma Naranjo grew up cooking with her mother and grandmother at Ohkay Owingeh, then called San Juan Pueblo, and she continues to ply the craft with an abundance of passion and pride. Her business, the Feasting Place, seems to do as much cooking as a dozen restaurants, offering classes on many aspects of traditional Pueblo food, catering for occasions as varied as weddings and a dinner at the Governor's Mansion, hosting meals in her home for up to forty guests, and selling some of the dried corn chicos that she and her husband, Hutch, raise and prepare themselves.

When Norma is not cooking for clients, she's likely to be cooking for family and friends. Since Hutch is from Santa Clara Pueblo, the couple celebrates twice as many feast days as most Pueblo families. The feasts keep both of their hornos busy baking bread, empanaditas, and more. Hutch lights the wood fires early in the morning, they sweep out the coals together after a couple of hours when the temperature is right, and Norma puts the food in the ovens, which together hold up to one hundred loaves of bread at the same time. Most people would need a nap by now, but with these preliminaries out of the way, Norma gets down to the rest of the cooking.

Guacamole

As an appetizer to serve at the table before a main course, guacamole functions much like a salad. New Mexicans developed a love for avocados by the early decades of the twentieth century and used them in many forms, but in more recent years, guacamole has soared in popularity to become the dominant dish of the field. We think it succeeds best as an exercise in simplicity, so we avoid extra ingredients that entice many cooks, such as garlic, tomatoes, and New Mexican chile.

Makes about 1½ cups

2 large ripe avocados (preferably Haas variety), chunked

2 tablespoons minced onion

1 fresh jalapeño or serrano chile, minced

½ teaspoon salt

juice of ½ lemon or lime

lettuce leaves or spears of romaine, optional

tortilla chips, optional

1. Mash avocados roughly in a medium bowl, leaving some chunks. Stir in the remaining ingredients.

2. Serve within about 30 minutes on top of lettuce leaves or spears of romaine, or with chips, or as a garnish to other dishes.

Burrell Tortillas

Simpler even than guacamole, this is just as sublime. Nothing more than a flour tortilla covered thoroughly with a gooey blend of melted cheese and green chile, the dish originated at Rancho de Chimayó and was named for a frequent patron, Mark Burrell. As far as we can recall, in scores of visits to the restaurant in the last four decade we've always ordered this for an appetizer.

Makes 2 tortillas

2 7- to 8-inch flour tortillas (page 138)

1 cup green chile sauce (page 26) or other green chile sauce

4 ounces (1 cup) shredded Colby or mild cheddar cheese

1. Preheat the oven to 350° F.

2. Cut each tortilla into 4 wedges. Arrange wedges in original tortilla shapes on a baking sheet or heatproof platter. Spoon chile sauce evenly over the reassembled tortillas and sprinkle cheese over all.

3. Bake for 5 to 6 minutes, until cheese is melted and a little bubbly. Serve piping hot. Eat with fingers or a fork, or a bit of each. It's drippy and delicious.

Quesadillas

The very same ingredients in the Burrell tortillas make a great quesadilla if you toast the tortillas, form them into a sandwich, and put a reduced quantity of the cheese and chile in between as the filling. Many New Mexicans make quesadillas like this today for a quick lunch or snack, but it's a food of expedience rather than heritage.

When early New Mexico cookbooks mention quesadillas, they usually refer to a dessert turnover. Margarita C. de Baca, in her *New Mexico Dishes* (1937), for example, mixes "fresh native cheese" with eggs, sugar, and milk, and uses it to fill circles of "regular pie crust dough" folded over, pinched, and baked. Only Cleofas M. Jaramillo comes close to our current sense of quesadillas, which she spells "quesadias." She rolls out biscuit dough into "thin, round tortillas," spreads them with fresh cheese, and folds them for baking on a griddle until browned on both sides.

4 *Meat and Chile Classics*

When Spain began colonizing the Americas, the diet in the mother country revolved around meat, wheat, and wine. The settlers, naturally, brought with them a taste for these goods, and a preference for them above other foods persisted for generations all over the Americas, including New Mexico. Native Americans introduced them to different fare, of course, and the colonists adopted much of it to varying degrees, but they seldom if ever voluntarily gave up the original trinity of staples.

In the case of wheat and wine, New Mexico settlers prepared and consumed them much like their ancestors did in Spain. They made bread as white and refined as they could afford and drank wine for both sacred and secular occasions. In contrast, the way they ate meat changed enormously over time, likely in gradual increments.

They still roasted or simmered meat, the main cooking methods of a hearth-based kitchen, but they lacked local sources for most seasonings except salt, onions, garlic, coriander, and cumin. Columbus and his crews had already mistaken chile as a kind of pepper plant, like the ones that produce black peppercorns, so it must have made imminent sense to try it as a flavoring agent. With experience, cooks perfected the idea and came to rely on it much more heavily than their counterparts in Mexico and other areas of the Americas, where different seasoning options usually existed.

The robust combination of meat and chile became the foundation of traditional New Mexico cooking as early as the eighteenth century. Many people today think of enchiladas, tamales, and similar dishes as the basic foods of the state, but those came to prominence later and owe their distinctive chile flavor to the previous development of local sauces hearty enough to mate with meat.

In the colonial era, meat meant mainly mutton, goat, and game, but our recipes reflect the contemporary preference for beef and pork.

Chile con Carne

This simple preparation is the essence of New Mexican food, and in its basics, perhaps the starting point in the evolution of dishes in this chapter. The name and inspiration are somewhat similar to the chili con carne developed later in Texas and spread from there across the country, but the New Mexico version gets its tang from a pure, pungent chile instead of a mild ancho powder spiked with other additives, and it never contains ground meat, beans, or the spaghetti found sometimes in Cincinnati versions. As early as 1916, at least one New Mexican, Alice Stevens Tipton, was already railing against these "spurious" versions that she called "a sloppy concoction unfit for the human stomach." Chile con carne can be served on its own, in a combination plate with other favorites, or as a part of dishes such as Stuffed Sopaipillas (page 100).

Serves 4 to 6

2 tablespoons vegetable oil

1½ pounds beef sirloin, in
    ½-inch cubes

2 garlic cloves, minced

¼ cup dried ground mild or
    medium New Mexican red
    chile

1½ cups water (divided use)

1 teaspoon salt

½ teaspoon crumbled dried
    Mexican oregano or marjoram

2 teaspoons cornstarch

1. Warm the oil in a large skillet over medium heat. Sauté the beef until brown on all sides. Add the garlic and cook for 1 minute, then stir in the chile and cook for about 1 minute more. Pour in 1¼ cups of the water, then add salt and oregano (or marjoram) and give it all a good stir. Simmer about 20 minutes, or until the beef is tender. If the mixture dries out while cooking before the beef is tender, stir in a little extra water.

2. Stir together the remaining water with cornstarch. Pour the mixture into the chile con carne and cook for about 5 more minutes, stirring frequently.

3. Serve warm or use in other preparations.

Variations: As in any preparation with red chile, some cooks start from Chile Caribe (page 22) in place of dried ground chile and water. For a lamb chile con carne, simply switch out the beef for sirloin or leg meat. For a version made with pork, see Katy's Chile con Carne in the recipe for Tostadas Compuestas, Estila de La Posta (page 92). Green chile renditions are less common but definitely tasty with either beef or pork; one simple approach is to substitute green chile sauce (page 26) for the red chile and water.

Carne Adovada

Carne adovada, as it's usually spelled today (originally carne adobada), always ranks among the fieriest New Mexico dishes. Like chile con carne, it is meat flavored with little more than pure chile, and perhaps because of this, few New Mexico restaurants offer both dishes. In the northern part of the state, professional kitchens overwhelmingly favor carne adovada, and in the south they usually serve chile con carne. It's an odd situation because both thrived as recognized classics around the state in the past, and they are clearly different from each other in elemental ways. At least for us and many other home cooks, we've got plenty of passion for both. Carne adovada can be presented simply on its own as the recipe suggests or can be enveloped in a flour tortilla as a burrito and topped with more chile and cheese. Some like it as a filling for enchiladas, stuffed sopaipillas, empanadas, or turnovers. As a breakfast eye-opener, it fires up eggs as a bacon substitute or as meat for a scramble or an omelet.

Serves 6 to 8

3 pounds pork shoulder, trimmed of fat and cut into 1½-inch cubes

Sauce

8 ounces (about 20 to 25) whole dried red New Mexican chiles, preferably Chimayó, stemmed, seeded, and rinsed

2 cups chicken or beef stock or water

1 medium onion, chunked

4 garlic cloves

2 teaspoons vinegar, preferably sherry or cider

2 teaspoons crumbled dried Mexican oregano or marjoram

1 teaspoon ground coriander, optional

1 teaspoon salt, or more to taste

shredded lettuce and chopped tomato, optional

1. Preheat the oven to 300° F. Grease a large, covered baking dish. Place the pork in the baking dish.

2. Prepare the sauce. Begin by placing the damp chiles in a layer on a baking sheet and toasting them in the oven for about 5 minutes, until they darken just a shade (they can have a little remaining moisture). Watch chiles carefully because they can scorch quickly. Remove them from the oven but leave the oven on. Cool chiles briefly, then break each into 2 or 3 pieces, discarding stems and most seeds.

3. Dump approximately half of the chiles into a blender with 1 cup of stock or water. Puree until you have a smooth, thick liquid but can see tiny even pieces of chile pulp suspended in it. Pour the mixture into the baking dish. Repeat with the remaining pods and stock, adding the rest of the sauce ingredients to the blender. Add mixture to the baking dish and stir the sauce together with the pork.

4. Cover the dish and bake at 300° F until the meat is quite tender and the sauce has cooked down, about 3 hours. If the sauce seems watery, return the dish to the oven uncovered and bake for an additional 15 to 30 minutes.

5. Serve hot, garnished if you wish with lettuce and tomato. Reheated leftovers are outstanding.

Working ahead: Carne adovada makes the perfect do-ahead dish. The uncooked pork can steep in the chile mixture for up to several days before baking. Once cooked, the dish can be cooled, refrigerated, and saved until the next day, or portions of it can be enjoyed over several days. Like many braised dishes, a reheating or two seems to make it even better.

Mary & Tito's

Mary and Tito Gonzales opened their small, down-to-earth café in 1963 just north of downtown Albuquerque on Fourth Street. Tito already had a reputation as a good home cook, but when he proposed the restaurant idea Mary responded cautiously, saying she wasn't going to tend any pots or wash any dishes. Tito agreed to handle the kitchen, and he trained his helpers so well that they took over seamlessly after their mentor died. Mary ran the front of the house and still does, now ably assisted by her daughter Antoinette Gonzales Knight.

Anything that can be made with carne adovada, from burritos to turnovers, excels. The chile rellenos are another highlight, and all of the other New Mexico dishes shine. The prestigious James Beard Foundation recognized the homespun quality by honoring Mary & Tito's in 2010 as an "America's Classic." Learning of this award, Governor Bill Richardson declared a Mary & Tito's Day across the state.

Lamb Shanks Adobo

Among the livestock the Spanish introduced to the Southwest, churro sheep thrived particularly well throughout the colonial era. A hardy breed known for rich meat, the churros gradually lost favor by the twentieth century and declined steadily in numbers until a recent revival stimulated by the Navajo Sheep Project and Ganados del Valle, a cooperative of northern New Mexico ranchers. You can use any kind of lamb in this dish, but if you find churro lamb at a farmers' market or specialty store, definitely give it a try.

Serves 4 or more

4 pounds lamb shanks, cut in 2-inch-thick slices by your butcher

½ cup ground dried mild to medium New Mexican red chile

2 cups lamb, chicken, or veal stock

15-ounce can crushed tomatoes with juice

1 medium onion, chopped

1 canned chipotle chile plus 1 teaspoon adobo sauce, optional

1 tablespoon sherry or cider vinegar

3 garlic cloves

1 teaspoon crumbled dried Mexican oregano or marjoram

1 teaspoon salt, or more to taste

2 bay leaves

minced onion and cilantro for garnish, optional

1. Preheat the oven to 300° F.

2. Mix together the lamb shanks and other ingredients in a Dutch oven or other heavy pan. Bake uncovered for about 3 hours. Stir up from the bottom after about 2 hours, then continue baking until the meat is tender and pulls easily away from the bones. If the sauce remains very thin, remove the lamb with a slotted spoon, place the pan over a stove burner, and reduce the sauce until it is thick enough to heavily coat a spoon. Then pour sauce over lamb.

3. Serve hot, garnished if you wish with onion and cilantro.

Working ahead: If you like, mix all of the ingredients together (as in step 2) and refrigerate overnight before baking. Plan on a few extra minutes in baking time. Making the dish entirely and then simply reheating it the following day works well, too.

Chicharrónes con Chile

A good batch of New Mexico chicharrónes is porcine perfection. Forget images of crinkly pork rinds, the junk food other people call chicharrónes. The New Mexico dish is a crispy morsel of meat fried slowly in its own fat. At a hog butchering in the late fall, called a *matanza* here, the pork contains bits of skin, but home versions usually don't. In both cases, the chicharrónes are party food, the highlight of a *matanza* or any other kind of celebration. Our friend Martín Leger, who grew up in Las Vegas, New Mexico, swears by the addition of milk to help brown and crisp his chicharrónes, an idea he credits to his brother Howard. Red chile tastes fine with the dish, but we prefer green and will often heap both it and the meat into a burrito. We sometimes sneak in a few chunks of fried potato when eating chicharrónes at breakfast, though Martín is not pleased with that notion. He's emphatic that chicharrónes are a delicacy and that anything other than chile is a distraction.

Serves 6

3 pounds fatty pork butt or shoulder, untrimmed, cut into strips about ½ by 2 inches (often labeled as meat for chicharrónes in New Mexico)

1 quart whole or 2% milk (as if you want to save on calories)

1 teaspoon salt, or more to taste

Chile Verde Table Relish (page 27)

1. Place the pork in a large Dutch oven or other deep heavy pan. Pour the milk over the meat. The milk should come to about the top of the pork. Add 1 teaspoon of salt.

2. Plan on a total cooking time of 1½ to 2½ hours. Cook over medium-low heat, stirring the mixture up from the bottom after 30 minutes and again after an hour. Quite a bit of fat will render from the pork so that after an hour or so the pork should be frying slowly in its fat as the liquid gradually evaporates.

3. In the second hour of cooking, stir every 10 minutes or so to make sure the meat cooks evenly throughout. Watch the chicharrónes carefully, stirring more and more frequently toward the end of the cooking so the meat doesn't burn. Chicharrónes are ready when the meat is richly brown, completely tender, and crispy chewy in spots. You will still have lots of strips of meat but also crumbly extra-crisp bits of meat and fat that separated during the stirring.

4. Drain with a slotted spoon and cool on paper towels. Sprinkle with more salt if you wish.

5. Serve with a generous quantity of green chile relish to eat with each bite.

Working ahead: Chicharrónes can be kept at room temperature for the rest of the day that they are made. If any remain, they can be bagged and refrigerated. To serve again, scatter on a baking sheet and reheat them for a few minutes in a 250° F oven.

West Las Vegas High School Cheer, circa 1975

Chicharrónes, chicharrónes,
Greasy, greasy, greasy,
We can beat the Cardinals,
Easy, easy, easy!

Carnitas

Much of the pork from a hog butchering that isn't cut into chicharrónes becomes carnitas ("little meats"), semi-crispy bits of kettle-cooked succulence. As with the previous recipe, some cooks add milk to enhance the browning and crisping. People who enjoy their carnitas extra crunchy may increase the amount of lard or vegetable oil by a tablespoon or so and fry the pork cubes until they are darker brown and beginning to shred. Other cooks finish off the carnitas by simmering them for a few minutes (no more) in a bath of red chile sauce. We prefer to serve red chile on the side to keep the liquid from diluting the crispiness of the meat. Carnitas can be eaten as a plated main dish or folded into tortillas.

Serves 6

4 garlic cloves

1 tablespoon ground dried mild to hot New Mexican red chile

2 teaspoons crumbled dried Mexican oregano

1 teaspoon salt

½ teaspoon freshly ground black pepper

2½ pounds pork butt (shoulder), cut into bite-size cubes, eliminating chunks of surface fat

¼ cup lard

¼ cup whole or 2% milk

1. With a mortar and pestle, mash together the garlic, red chile, oregano, salt, and pepper. Dump the mixture into a medium-size bowl. Toss the pork cubes with the spice mixture. Let sit at room temperature for 20 to 30 minutes.

2. Warm the lard in a Dutch oven or other deep heavy pan over medium-high heat. Spoon the pork into the hot lard, watching out for the inevitable splatters, and sear the meat. Reduce the heat to a bare simmer and cover the pan. Cook the pork for 1 hour, stirring the mixture at 20-minute intervals. Uncover the pork and stir in the milk. Raise the heat to medium high. Simmer until most of the liquid has evaporated, scraping the mixture up from the bottom. After about 10 minutes the pork cubes will be browned and lightly crisped, while tender and moist inside.

3. Remove the carnitas with a slotted spoon and serve.

Roque's Beef Carnitas

Pork is the most common meat for carnitas in New Mexico and the rest of the borderlands, but many cooks also make a stellar rendition with beef. This is the popular version that Roque Garcia and his wife, Mona Cavalli, have served for decades from their street cart on the Santa Fe Plaza. The couple credits Roque's mother for the original home recipe, which Roque recommends duplicating in other home kitchens in the following manner. He calls for an overnight marinating for the meat, but we have had good results with as little as a half-hour soak when rushed.

Serves 4

1½ pounds boneless sirloin or
    top round steak, cut across the
    grain into ⅛-inch strips

1 tablespoon vegetable oil

1 large onion, sliced thin

5 fresh mild New Mexican
    green chiles, sliced into very
    thin rounds

4 thick flour tortillas (page 138),
    warmed

Marinade

6 tablespoons vegetable oil

6 tablespoons soy sauce

1 tablespoon crumbled dried
    Mexican oregano

4 garlic cloves, minced

Mona's Salsa

2 medium tomatoes, diced

1 small onion, chopped

2 to 6 fresh jalapeños, chopped
    fine

2 tablespoons minced cilantro,
    optional

2 garlic cloves, minced

salt, optional

For marinade

1. The night before you plan to cook, place the beef strips in a gallon Ziplock bag. Combine the marinade ingredients in a bowl and pour it over the beef. Refrigerate covered for as long as you can manage, up to 24 hours.

For salsa

1. The day you plan to cook, stir together the salsa ingredients in a bowl. Add salt if you wish, keeping in mind that the soy sauce in the meat marinade gives a good bit of salty tang to the dish. Refrigerate until ready to serve.

Assembly

1. Drain the beef strips, discarding the marinade.

2. In a large heavy wok or cast-iron skillet, warm half of the oil over high heat until it just begins to smoke. Add half of the beef and stir-fry, tossing almost constantly, until browned well, about 2 minutes. Repeat with the remaining oil and meat. Transfer the meat to a plate as the strips get deeply colored.

3. Reduce the heat under the skillet to medium and add the onion and chile. Cook until softened and charred in a few spots, stirring almost constantly. Return the meat to the skillet and toss with the vegetables.

4. Using tongs, lift about ¼ of the meat mixture from the skillet, getting a balanced mix of meat and vegetables. Allow excess juices to drip back into the skillet. Fill a tortilla. Repeat with remaining beef mixture and tortillas. Top with salsa and serve right away. Pick the tortilla up and fold it upward like a taco to devour.

Working ahead: In addition to marinating the beef a day ahead, you can slice the onions and chiles and wrap them tightly to store overnight in the refrigerator.

Albóndigas in Red Chile

When the Museum of New Mexico Press made an advanced announcement about the publication of this book and requested recipe submissions, Diana Moya Lujan of Santa Fe shared this treat with us. She explained, "Each time I make albóndigas I feel a connection to my maternal grandmother, Aurelia Romero Luna, who I never met. She grew up in the Rio Puerco area and died before I was born. However, I was always in the kitchen with my mother, Ethel Luna Moya, and she passed on many of Grandmother's recipes. The albóndigas were a special dish, cooked for important occasions and for the holidays. Mom's brother was in the CIA from the mid-1940s through the early 1970s, and when he came for a visit Mom always made her mother's albóndigas."

Serves 6 to 8

Aurelia Romero Luna's Red Chile Caribe

5 to 6 ounces (12 to 15 pods) whole New Mexican red chile pods

water

1 garlic clove

1 teaspoon salt, or more to taste

Albóndigas

1½ pounds lean (not extra-lean) ground beef

½ small onion, minced

1 garlic clove, minced

1 large egg

½ cup saltine cracker crumbs (about 10 crackers)

½ teaspoon salt

For chile caribe

1. Remove the stems and seeds from the chile pods. Rinse the pods in a large bowl of water. Drain and discard the water. Place the pods in a saucepan and cover them with water. Bring to a boil and cook for about 5 minutes. Let stand for 5 to 10 minutes, then discard water.

2. Place half of the pods in a blender with enough fresh water to cover and blend to a good liquefied state. Pour into a bowl. Add the remaining pods and garlic clove to the blender and again cover with water and blend. Add to the remaining chile, sprinkle in salt, and stir to combine.

For albóndigas

1. Work all ingredients together in a mixing bowl with your fingers. Don't over-work once blended. Form meatballs about the size of hefty walnuts (approximately 24), wetting your fingers with cold water if the meat mixture is sticking to you.

2. Arrange albóndigas in a large heavy skillet and cook over medium-low heat, turning frequently so they brown but do not crisp. When albóndigas have lost their raw color on all sides, pour in red chile caribe (it will look just like meat-balls in spaghetti sauce). Continue cooking for 20 to 25 minutes, stirring occasionally, until the sauce has cooked down by about ⅓. Reduce the heat if the mixture begins to boil up. Season with more salt if you wish.

3. Spoon the albóndigas into broad shallow bowls. Ladle generous portions of sauce around the meatballs and serve.

Working ahead: Red chile caribe can be prepared up to several days ahead and stored in the refrigerator. The albóndigas mixture can be combined a day ahead, formed into meatballs, and arranged on a greased baking sheet. In either case, cover tightly with plastic wrap before refrigerating.

Chile Rellenos "Balls"

Like any living cuisine, New Mexico food flaunts contradictions. A delightful example is this dish, typically called just "chile rellenos," even though the chiles are not "stuffed" at all. Instead, these are batter-dipped beef-and-chile finger food, likely created as an expedient way to mimic the flavor of a meaty rellenos when serving crowds gathered for weddings and holiday meal celebrations. We had read about them, but never prepared them until after our first meeting with our publisher, Anna Gallegos, who reminisced about the dish with a wistful smile. Along with Anna, nearly everyone else who suggested them to us has family ties to the center third of the state in the Rio Abajo area. In Anna's family, her paternal grandfather, Pete Gallegos, made an especially tasty version, but he was tutored by her grandmother Gloria Miera Gallegos, who was the family's best all-around cook. "Daddy Pete," as he was known to all of his grandchildren, was born in Magdalena and "Nana" in San Antonio, both towns close to Socorro. These can be eaten as a part of a sit-down meal, but they also make great snacks or party nibbles.

Makes about 30 2-inch chiles rellenos

Rellenos Balls	Batter
1¾-pound slab beef chuck	3 large eggs, separated
salt	½ cup all-purpose flour
2 to 4 garlic cloves	
1 to 1½ cups beef stock	½ cup all-purpose flour, for dredgiing
1 cup chopped roasted mild, medium, or hot New Mexican green chile, fresh or thawed frozen	vegetable oil or lard, for deep-frying
1 to 2 tablespoons all-purpose flour (if needed)	

For rellenos balls

1. Warm a Dutch oven or other large, heavy pot over high heat. Salt the meat and then place it in the skillet and brown on both sides, about 5 minutes total. Scatter garlic cloves around meat. Pour in stock and scrape up browned bits from the bottom. Reduce the heat to medium low, cover, and simmer about 1½ hours, until tender. Check after about 1 hour and if the liquid is in danger of evaporating completely pour in a few tablespoons of hot water. Let the meat cool in the pan liquid, and when it's cool enough to handle discard the fat and pull meat into at least 6 chunks. Reduce remaining cooking liquid to about 2 tablespoons.

2. Chop together the meat, garlic cloves, and cooking liquid in a food processor, pulsing just until the meat is chopped uniformly. Add the chile, and pulse in several short bursts until the chile is mixed in evenly. The mixture should be

Better Than Butter

Into the early decades of the twentieth century, many farm women across the country made and sold butter as a way to supplement household income. Stella Hatch, an early Anglo settler in the Mesilla Valley, proved once again the observation of territorial governor Lew Wallace, who said, "Every calculation based on experience elsewhere fails in New Mexico."

Shortly after she arrived in the state, Hatch whipped some of her excess milk into butter and took it to a nearby store to sell, as she had done for years in her former home. The shopkeeper stunned her by saying that none of his clients bought butter, but they were constantly in need of lard for cooking local dishes. As Joan Jensen relates in her essay "Farm Women in New Mexico, 1920–1940," Hatch adeptly switched to animal fats and ended up with a profitable business producing lard.

fairly finely chopped, but pieces of the chile should still be visible. The meat and chile mixture should be well seasoned. Add salt if you wish. Check the texture of the mixture. If it holds together when compacted tightly, it's ready. If not, add 1 tablespoon of flour and pulse once more until flour is mixed in. Test again. If not holding together, add up to 1 more tablespoon of flour and pulse again.

3. Form ovals of the meat and chile mixture with your hands, making them about 2 inches long but about 1 inch in diameter. Arrange on a baking sheet. Refrigerate briefly while you ready the batter and oil.

For batter
1. Beat the egg whites with a mixer until soft peaks form. Stop the mixer, add the egg yolks and 2 tablespoons of flour, then mix again just until combined.

Assembly
1. Warm 3 to 4 inches of oil in a broad saucepan or deep skillet over medium heat to 350° F. Place ½ cup of flour in a shallow bowl. Arrange several thicknesses of paper towels within easy reach of the stove.

2. Dredge balls first in flour, then in the egg batter. Your first few may look a bit free-form rather than like perfect spheres. Experiment to see if you find batter-dipping easiest with fingers, using a small spoon as a scoop, or spearing the balls with a thin-tined fork.

3. Gently add balls to the oil, a few at a time. The balls will sink to the bottom, then rise back up to the top of the oil. Fry until the batter coating is puffed, golden brown, and lightly crisp, 4 to 5 minutes. Nudge balls around a bit with a slotted spoon as needed to fry evenly. Using the slotted spoon, remove the balls and drain on paper towels. Continue until all chile rellenos balls are fried, adjusting the oil temperature as needed to keep it steady. Eat warm.

Working ahead: Though they sound like something you'd probably have to eat immediately, these chiles rellenos were typically made ahead in big batches, cooled, then stored in paper-lined coffee cans to enjoy at room temperature over a few days. It was common to toss a few in pockets or saddlebags when hunting, fishing, or working cattle. You may not be headed out to the woods or corral, but you can divide the advance preparation into steps. Cook the beef one day and shred it, or go ahead and chop it with the chile and form it into balls, refrigerating overnight. Then whisk up the batter and fry shortly before you plan to serve the chiles rellenos.

Variations: In some families, the meat and chile mixture would have a tablespoon or more of sugar or brown sugar mixed into it along with raisins and occasionally nuts, more like a Mexican holiday picadillo. Other cooks intensify the sweetness, serving them with a sugar syrup for dunking at the table or drizzling the fried balls with sugar syrup before offering them to guests. For a crisper, almost crunchy surface, fry the batter-dipped balls at 375° F for 3 to 4 minutes. Some families opt for a rounder shape to their rellenos balls. Form golf-ball-size rounds, then dunk in flour and batter as above, and fry at 350° F for about 4 minutes.

Green Chile Cheeseburgers

In New Mexico and the rest of the country, the popularity of the hamburger dates back to the early days of drive-in eateries and roadside cafés. A number of places from that era claim to have invented the state's iconic version of the burger, but it seems likely to have evolved naturally in many kitchens about the same time. If you start with fresh chiles, simply char them on the grill before you cook the burgers. Two keys to success are draining the chile well and using a bun sturdy enough to contain the fixings.

Serves 6

Burgers

2¼ to 2½ pounds freshly ground beef chuck

1 teaspoon salt

1 teaspoon freshly milled black pepper

6 burger-size slices mild cheddar, American, or Monterey Jack cheese, at room temperature

1½ to 2 cups chopped roasted mild to hot New Mexican green chile, fresh or thawed frozen, warmed

Trimmings

6 large sturdy hamburger buns (toast at the side of the grill, if you wish)

ketchup or mayonnaise

6 thick slices large red-ripe tomatoes (skip them out of season)

crisp iceberg lettuce leaves and slices of mild onion, dill pickles, or crisp cooked bacon, optional

For the burgers

1. See How to Grill Like a Pro (at right). Fire up the grill for a 2-level fire capable of cooking first on high heat (1 to 2 seconds with the hand test) and then on medium heat (4 to 5 seconds with the hand test).

2. Mix together the ground chuck, salt, and pepper. *Gently* form the mixture into six patties ½- to ¾-inch thick. Your patties should hold together but avoid handling them any longer than necessary.

3. Grill the burgers uncovered over high heat for 1½ minutes per side. Move the burgers to medium heat and rotate a half turn for crisscross grill marks. Do not—DO NOT—mash the burgers with the spatula. Cook for 3½ to 4 minutes longer, then turn once more and cover each burger with cheese. Cook another 3½ to 4 minutes for medium doneness, a bare hint of pink at the center of each crusty richly browned burger.

TIP

How to Grill Like a Pro

• Leave the grill cover open for the short time it takes to grill your food.

• Burgers and steaks come out best when grilled over a hot fire first to sear the surface and then a medium fire to finish cooking to desired doneness.

• The most effective way to measure the cooking temperature is really the simplest—the time-honored hand test. Place your hand a couple of inches above the cooking grate and count the number of seconds until the heat of the fire forces you to pull away. One to two seconds signifies hot, three seconds denotes medium high, and four to five seconds for medium.

• On a gas grill with three or more burners, you can set burners to keep a hot fire and a medium fire going simultaneously. On a smaller gas grill, simply turn the heat down at the appropriate point.

• With a charcoal grill, arrange the fuel in two different cooking areas, with a single layer of coals for medium heat and coals piled up two to three deep for the hot fire.

Assembly

1. Smear buns with ketchup or mayo. (We think it's best to pick one because too many flavors begin to interfere with the chile.) If you're using tomato, or any of the other optional toppings, arrange on each bun next. Follow with cheese-covered burgers. Spoon chile over each. Crown with bun tops.

2. Eat burgers hot from the grill, squeezing buns gently to mingle all the juices.

Variations: Most green chile cheeseburgers are pretty straightforward affairs, and often it's best to mess less with the tried-and-true. However, the burger crowned king at the cook-off staged at the 2010 New Mexico State Fair broke the rule artfully. ABQ Brew Pub's chef Ruben Rodarte tempura-fried his green chile. If you want to give that a whirl, see Green Chile Tempura (page 122). Mesilla's Double Eagle, home of the world's largest green chile cheeseburger, a platter-size behemoth, goes a little farther with fried topping options, too, with a chile rellenos–capped burger. The most common variation on the classic burger is to morph it into a tortilla burger, wrapping it in a flour tortilla, and plating it seam-side down before blanketing the whole package in chile sauce.

Steak Dunigan

Steaks smothered in chile abound in New Mexico restaurants, but this is probably the most famous version, created long ago by Rosalea Murphy during her fifty-year tenure as the proprietor at the Pink Adobe in Santa Fe. She named it after a regular patron, Pat Dunigan, who loved green chile on his steak. Her kitchen made the dish from this recipe, which she kindly shared with us once. The Char Crust dry rub she specified isn't difficult to find today, but in a pinch you can substitute a generous seasoning with coarse salt or smoked salt and freshly milled pepper. If you can find prime-grade steak at a real meat market, it will be worth a splurge. Rosalea said the steaks could be pan-seared or grilled, but we always opt for the latter.

Serves 2 at the Pink Adobe but can easily serve 4 or more at home

Steaks

1 to 1½ tablespoons Original Hickory Grilled Char Crust (available in the spice section of some supermarkets or from www.charcrust.com)

2 14- to 16-ounce New York strip steaks, 1 to 1¼ inches thick

Rosalea's Green Chile Sauce

2 tablespoons olive oil

1 small onion, finely chopped

1 cup chopped roasted mild to medium-hot New Mexican green chile, fresh or thawed frozen

1 teaspoon minced cilantro, optional

½ teaspoon crumbled dried Mexican oregano

½ teaspoon salt

Mushroom Topping

¼ cup unsalted butter

4 large button mushrooms, sliced thin

For steaks

1. About 30 to 45 minutes before cooking time, rub the Char Crust into all sides of the steaks. Let them sit at room temperature.

For sauce

1. Warm the oil in a medium saucepan over medium heat. Stir in the onion and sauté until soft, 5 to 7 minutes. Stir in the remaining ingredients. Cook about 5 minutes more, until heated through. Keep warm. Add a little water if it thickens beyond sauce consistency.

For mushroom topping

1. Heat butter in a small skillet until melted. Add mushrooms and sauté until soft, about 5 minutes. Keep warm.

Assembly

1. See How to Grill Like a Pro (page 66). Fire up a grill for a 2-level fire capable of cooking first on high heat (1 to 2 seconds with the hand test) and then on medium (4 to 5 seconds with the hand test).

2. Grill the steaks over high heat for 2 minutes per side. Move the steaks to medium heat, turning them again, and continue grilling for 2½ to 3 minutes per side for medium-rare doneness. Turn the steaks a minimum of 3 times, but more often if juice begins to form on the surface. Rotate a half-turn each time for crisscross grill marks.

3. For 2 diners, arrange steaks on plates and spoon half of the mushrooms over each steak. Spoon chile sauce evenly over the steaks. If serving more diners, let steaks sit for 5 minutes, then slice thickly and arrange on plates. Spoon chile sauce equally over all portions, followed by mushrooms and butter. Serve.

Working ahead: The chile sauce can be made a day ahead.

Green Chile Stew

A bowl of comfort, green chile stew always strikes us as much greater than the sum of its humble parts. Like many dishes featuring green chile, this rose in popularity substantially after home freezing of food extended the lifespan of green pods beyond their short season. Some cooks add thickeners like cornstarch or flour or use baking potatoes that yield the same result when they partially crumble and dissolve during cooking. In our view, the stew is amply hearty without thickeners, needing nothing more with it than a stack of warm flour tortillas or squares of corn bread.

Serves 8

1½ to 1¾ pounds beef chuck or pork butt (shoulder), cut in ½-inch cubes

2 medium onions, diced

4 garlic cloves, minced

1 to 1¼ pounds red waxy potatoes, peeled or unpeeled, and diced

5 cups beef or chicken stock

1½ tablespoons salt, or more to taste

3 cups chopped roasted mild to medium New Mexican green chile, fresh or thawed frozen

1 cup corn kernels, fresh or frozen, 1 cup carrot chunks, or 1 diced red bell pepper, optional

1. Sear the meat in a Dutch oven or large heavy saucepan over medium-high heat until it browns and liquid accumulated from the meat mostly evaporates. Stir in the onions and garlic and cook for several minutes, until the onions become translucent. Pour in stock and scrape the mixture up from the bottom to loosen browned bits. Sprinkle in the salt, reduce the heat to a low simmer, and cook uncovered for 1¼ hours.

2. Stir in the chile and any of the optional ingredients and continue cooking for another 45 minutes to 1 hour, until the meat is quite tender, the vegetables are soft, and the flavors have blended together.

3. Ladle into bowls and serve hot.

Working ahead: Like many stews, this becomes especially nice when made a day or two ahead. Simply reheat and serve.

Variations: Molly Manzanares, co-owner of Shepherd's Lamb in Tierra Amarilla, makes stew with her delectable pasture-raised lamb. As you might guess, her stew is richer in meat than our version and relegates other ingredients to a support role. To 1 pound of lamb stew meat, Molly uses ¼ cup of both onion and green chile, and a medium tomato or potato depending on the season.

Bueno Foods

When they returned from World War II, the Baca brothers decided to go into business together in their hometown of Albuquerque. They scraped together enough money to open a neighborhood grocery, the Ace Food Store. The Bacas made a modest living, particularly after adding take-out sales of their mother's traditional cooking, but the arrival of chain supermarkets made for tough competition.

Then inspiration struck in the early 1950s, when home freezers became the rage. Why not take their food heritage and preserve it in the new way? Why not roast chile over open flames, as had always been done, and then freeze it to enjoy all year? The Baca brothers founded Bueno Foods in 1951 to pursue this vision, inventing the equipment for commercial roasting and the techniques needed for manufacturing and distribution.

Bueno has grown into one of the largest Hispano businesses in the country, with approximately 150 products, but it's still a family operation. Jacqueline Baca, the daughter of one of the original brothers, has served as president for more than two decades, guiding the company through three major expansions. Bueno is a big enterprise but deeply rooted in New Mexico soil.

Sirloin Green Chile Stew

After a long and distinguished military career, Eloy Zamora retired in northern New Mexico. His grandson Arik Zamora, now a Taos chef, fondly remembers his childhood visits to New Mexico, when his grandfather made kettles of this green chile stew. The cooking inspired Arik's interest in becoming a chef, and those visits to Taos solidified his interest in settling down there. He now serves a version of the stew on his menu at the Gorge Bar & Grill. He likes to heat accompanying tortillas over a stovetop flame and char them just a bit before serving them piping hot. Because tender sirloin is the meat of choice for this stew, it can be ready much faster than the previous version, which keeps the flavor of each of the stew's components more distinct, too. You can cut down on the hearty measure of bacon drippings, but they do enhance the lean sirloin.

Serves 8

1 tablespoon vegetable oil

1 teaspoon salt, or more to taste

½ teaspoon black pepper, or more to taste

2 pounds beef sirloin, in ¾-inch cubes

2 quarts water

1 cup diced carrots

1 cup diced onion

1 cup peeled and diced red waxy potatoes

6 garlic cloves, minced

4 cups chopped roasted mild, medium, or hot New Mexican green chile, fresh or thawed frozen

2 tablespoons to ¼ cup bacon drippings

shredded mild cheddar or Monterey Jack cheese, optional

1. Warm the oil in a large saucepan over high heat. Stir salt and pepper into the oil, then add the beef. When the meat loses its raw color, add the water and scrape up the browned bits from the bottom. Stir in the carrots, onion, potatoes, garlic, chile, and bacon fat.

2. Reduce the heat and simmer until beef and vegetables are tender, about 30 minutes.

3. Ladle the stew into bowls. If you like, scatter cheese over each bowl immediately. Serve right away.

Red Chile Stew

Up through the early 1990s, if you wanted to know what was happening in Hatch, New Mexico, or even in Santa Fe, the state capital, all you had to do was hang out in the town's famed Dora's Café. We never got Dora's recipe for her version of this dish, but this is as similar as we can make it from memory.

Serves 8

2 tablespoons vegetable oil

2 pounds beef chuck roast, cut in ½-inch cubes

2 medium onions, chopped

4 garlic cloves, minced

4 cups beef stock, or more as needed

¾ cup ground dried mild to medium New Mexican red chile

2 teaspoons salt

1¼ teaspoons crumbled dried Mexican oregano or marjoram

2 cups cooked whole pinto beans, such as Frijoles de Olla (page 126), drained

1 large russet potato, cut in ½-inch cubes

chopped onions

shredded mild cheddar cheese

1. Warm the oil in a Dutch oven or small stockpot over high heat and sear the meat. Add the onions and garlic and sauté until the onions turn translucent. Pour in the stock and scrape browned bits up from the bottom. Stir in the chile, salt, and oregano (or marjoram), and reduce the heat to very low. Cover.

2. Cook for 2 hours, stirring every half hour or so. Then mix in the beans and potato and continue cooking, uncovered, for an additional 30 minutes or until the meat and potato are both very tender and the consistency has gone from soupy to thicker and more stew-like. Stir up from the bottom at least a couple of times during the last few minutes of cooking to make sure the mixture doesn't stick.

3. Serve steaming hot in bowls topped with onion and cheese.

Variations: Another great red chile stew comes from legendary San Ildefonso Pueblo potter Blue Corn. Prior to her success as a potter, Blue Corn worked as a housekeeper for the director of the Manhattan Project, J. Robert Oppenheimer. A cookbook published by the Los Alamos Historical Society, *Savoring the Past* (2001), featured her stew. Toast 6 red chile pods, discard the seeds and stems, and puree them in a blender with 1 tablespoon of flour and ¾ cup of water. In a large saucepan, simmer together 2 pounds of pork loin cut in 1-inch cubes with 3 cups of water for 45 minutes. Cut 1 pound of red waxy potatoes in 1-inch cubes and chop 2 large onions, and add them to the pan. When the potatoes are nearly tender, pour in the red chile mixture and cook for another 5 to 10 minutes.

Previous page: *Young squash marks the beginning of the summer growing season in Rio en Medio in Northern New Mexico, 2008. All photos by Sharon Stewart.*

Left: *Hearts of rainbow chard El Guique, 2004.*

Top left: *Maya Szapowski sniffs a mushroom from a hunt at the Hummingbird Community, Cleveland, NM, 2010.*

Top right: *A bolete mushroom found in the forests near Cleveland, NM, 2010.*

Left: *Priscilla Bunker buys carrots from Kathleen Dudley at the Mora Farmers Market held on the grounds of the Cleveland Roller Mill, Cleveland, NM, 2008.*

Previous spreads: Tomás Sanchez stirs a pot of chicharrones over a wood fire at the Romero Family Reunion held on the banks of the Mora River in Golondrinas, NM, 2010.

Dancers delight at traditional Northern New Mexico music played by the Jenny Vincent Trio at the Cleveland Roller Mill Fest, Cleveland, NM, 2002.

Fall harvesters in El Guique, north of Española, along the banks of the Rio Grande, 2004.

5 Enchiladas, Tamales, and Other Traditional Favorites

Until the twentieth century, few firsthand accounts of cooking or eating in New Mexico mentioned enchiladas, tacos, tamales, or other similar dishes. Most of them surely existed in a reasonably recognizable form before then because many of their basic elements—tortillas, chile, beans, cheese, and more—were clearly important in the colonial past.

It seems likely that increasing contact with Mexico after the end of the Spanish era in 1821 encouraged expanded recognition and popularity for these humble but richly flavorful foods. They weren't simply imported dishes, however, because New Mexico versions in almost all cases differ substantially from any counterparts in Mexico or other parts of the Southwest. The reliance on pure chile in the seasoning is the main distinguishing feature, but there are other singular characteristics as well, such as the frequent use of blue masa in tortillas.

Whatever the circumstances of their evolution, most of the dishes in this chapter were established favorites by the time New Mexico attained statehood in 1912. With the exception of tacos, burritos, and a few specialized variations on other foods, everything here made a prominent appearance in the earliest cookbooks published in the new state. Even the latecomers began showing up regularly within the next several decades in a distinctly New Mexican style.

While these classics might not be the first foods of New Mexico historically, they are culinary treasures of the first order in the hearts and minds of most residents today. Almost everyone in the state would rank one or more of the dishes below among their main reasons for living here.

Stacked Red Enchiladas

The ultimate New Mexico enchilada, this molten melding of chile, cheese, and corn tortillas can never be dismissed as ordinary food, even by people who find it heavy or overpowering. Its heritage reflects the state, being both Hispano and Pueblo in temper and probably origin, perhaps a little more of the latter when a cook uses blue corn tortillas. The term "enchilada" characterizes the way the dish is made, by dipping or drenching the tortillas in chile. Unlike in most places, in New Mexico the tortillas are generally stacked rather than rolled unless they are sharing a plate with other foods, when rolling minimizes the space they take. Stacking the enchilada in several layers tends to make it an entire main course rather than a component of a combination plate. If you are serving multiple people, you can make four or more stacked enchiladas on a baking sheet if you wish, then carefully transfer the stacks, after broiling, from the baking sheet to serving dishes.

Makes 1 serving (multiply by the number of servings you wish)

vegetable oil for pan frying

3 blue corn tortillas (page 137)

¾ cup red chile sauce (page 23 or 24), warmed

2 teaspoons minced onion

4 ounces shredded mild cheddar, Colby, or Monterey Jack cheese

1. Heat the broiler. (If the broiler has multiple heat settings, use the lowest.)

2. Heat ½ to 1 inch of oil in a small skillet until the oil ripples. With tongs, dunk each tortilla in oil long enough for it to go limp, a matter of seconds. Don't let the tortilla turn crisp. Drain and repeat with the remaining tortillas.

3. On a heatproof plate, layer the first tortilla with 1 teaspoon onion and ⅓ of the chile sauce and cheese. Repeat for the second layer. Top with the third tortilla, then add the remaining chile sauce and sprinkle the remaining cheese over all.

4. Broil the enchilada until the cheese melts. Serve piping hot.

The Shed

Among the best places to enjoy stacked red enchiladas with blue corn tortillas is the Shed in Santa Fe, where they've been "the number four" on the menu for decades. One of the keys to the winning formula is the daily grinding of the chile out behind the restaurant by Chef Josh Carswell.

Josh is part of the third generation of Carswells at the helm of the family business, which began in 1953 in a former burro shed on Burro Alley. On the retirement of the founders, Thornton and Polly Carswell, the family moved the restaurant a few blocks across downtown to Palace Avenue, locating it in a wonderful adobe hacienda dating to 1692.

Around the same time, the Shed began specializing in northern New Mexico chile dishes, which weren't on the original menu featuring salads, sandwiches, and plate lunches. The restaurant soon won fame for the new fare, which eventually earned it a James Beard Foundation Award as an "America's Classic" of timeless appeal.

Variations: Now that green chile is much less of a seasonal product than it used to be, an increasing number of cooks like to flavor cheese enchiladas with a green chile sauce (page 26). Many recipes call for longhorn cheese, which has nothing to do with the longhorn cattle of the Southwest. The term refers generally to mild cheese pressed into a long log, generally Colby or cheddar, then sold in half-moon or full-moon slices. Before commercially made fresh cheeses were regularly available, New Mexico—like most rural areas of the country—experienced a period when shelf-stable Velveeta processed cheese was the go-to product. If you came of age in the first half of the twentieth century, you may still think of it as the taste of childhood dishes. Prior to that, folks would have used their own—or a neighbor's—creamy fresh goat cheese, not a bad choice these days, either. *Queso de cabra's* tanginess is a good foil with the richness of the red chile sauce, but it doesn't melt as fully as the cheeses used commonly today. A half-and-half blend of mild fresh goat cheese with cheddar, Colby, or Monterey Jack gives you the best of both worlds.

Rolled Green Chile Chicken Enchiladas

Despite being a relatively recent addition to the New Mexican food repertoire, these enchiladas rival the popularity of cheese versions today. Though the chile sauce often contains bits of pork or beef, those meats rarely serve as enchilada fillings in New Mexico except in carne adovada variations. Freshly poached chicken makes an especially appealing filling, but you can also use instead about 3 cups of shredded roast chicken or other cooked chicken.

Serves 6

Filling

3 individual bone-in skin-on chicken breasts or a combination of 2 breasts with 2 thighs

3 cups chicken stock

½ onion, chopped

3 garlic cloves, minced

¼ teaspoon salt

vegetable oil for frying

12 corn tortillas

3 cups green chile sauce (page 23 or 24) or other green chile sauce

¼ cup minced onion

8 ounces (2 cups) shredded Monterey Jack, asadero, or mild cheddar cheese, or a combination

8 ounces cream cheese, cut while cold into about 24 small cubes

For filling

1. In a large saucepan, bring the chicken and other ingredients just to a boil. Reduce the heat to a low simmer and poach the chicken until cooked through and very tender, 25 to 30 minutes. Let the chicken cool for a few minutes in the liquid.

2. Drain the chicken and when cool enough to handle shred it into bite-size pieces. (Save the cooking liquid for soups or sauces.)

The Whole Enchilada Fiesta

The recipe calls for 750 pounds of stone-ground corn, 175 gallons of vegetable oil, 75 gallons of red chile sauce, 175 pounds of grated cheese, and 50 pounds of chopped onions. The ground corn is used to make masa for three tortillas, each of which requires fourteen people to carry it from the tortilla press to the cooking vat and on to the serving plate.

It's the world's largest flat enchilada, made in the stacked New Mexico style. Robert V. Estrada, the founder of the Whole Enchilada Fiesta in Las Cruces, cooks one each year as the highlight of the late-September festival using equipment he designed specifically for the purpose. He personally ladles on the chile and spreads the cheese and onions. The full process takes almost three hours, plenty of time for the spectators to whet their appetites for a free sample.

Assembly

1. Preheat the oven to 350° F. Grease a large baking dish. Spread about ¼ cup of the green chile sauce thinly in the baking dish.

2. Heat ½ to 1 inch of oil in a small skillet until the oil ripples. With tongs, dunk each tortilla in the oil long enough for it to go limp, a matter of seconds. Don't let the tortilla turn crisp. Repeat with the remaining tortillas. Blot with paper towels if you wish.

3. Dip a tortilla into the chile sauce. Top it with about ¼ cup of chicken, a couple of teaspoons of onion, a couple of cubes of cream cheese, and about a tablespoon of shredded cheese. Roll up the tortilla snugly but not tightly. Transfer the enchilada to the baking dish. Repeat with the rest of the tortillas and filling. Top the enchiladas with any remaining onion and pour the remaining sauce evenly over them. Scatter the rest of the cheese over the top.

4. Bake for about 20 minutes, until the enchiladas are heated through and the sauce and cheese are bubbly. Serve right away.

Working ahead: The chicken filling can be prepared a day or two ahead or frozen for up to two months.

Variations: Ramona Sakiestewa, the renowned textile artist of Hopi ancestry, prepared a version of these enchiladas for a party back in the early 1980s that both of us remember to this day. Her scrumptious recipe, which appeared once in *Sunset* magazine, calls for both cream cheese and cream in the filling, and a sauce made with 3 cups of pureed tomatillos flavored with enough chile to tingle the tongue. Albuquerque's beloved M & J Sanitary Tortilla Factory, unfortunately closed now, fixed some of the best carne adovada enchiladas we've had. To make a similar version, follow the general directions in this recipe using about 3 cups of shredded very tender carne adovada for the filling. Switch to red chile sauce, instead of green, and skip the cream cheese.

Green Chile Chicken Enchilada Casserole

Cheryl grew up in Illinois, the daughter of Republican parents. One day her father brought home a congressional Republicans cookbook, a gift of his local representative. Fascinated by cookbooks even at an early age, Cheryl took a pass on the moose Swiss steak from Alaska and even the Chinese peas from Hawaii. She zeroed in on an enchilada recipe with green chiles contributed by then-Congressman Manuel Lujan Jr., of the faraway Land of Enchantment. The recipe and the place sounded really exotic to the flatlander. Congressman (and later cabinet secretary) Lujan's recipe, which he admits actually comes from his wife, Jean, the cook in the family, is a simple casserole-style preparation. Complete with that old favorite cream of chicken soup, it's still popular in the state today for potlucks and other parties. The Lujans buy their chile for this and other dishes from the Farmers' Market store on Eubank in Albuquerque.

Serves 6 to 8

11- to 12-ounce can or box of condensed cream of chicken soup

1 cup half-and-half or canned evaporated milk

vegetable oil for frying

1 dozen corn tortillas

2 cups shredded cooked chicken (page 76)

1 cup chopped roasted mild to medium New Mexican green chile, fresh or thawed frozen, or more to taste

4 ounces (1 cup) shredded Colby or mild cheddar cheese

2 ounces (½ cup) shredded Monterey Jack cheese

¼ to ½ cup finely chopped onion

1. Preheat the oven to 350° F. Grease a large shallow baking dish. Stir together the soup and half-and-half (or evaporated milk) in a small bowl.

2. Heat ½ to 1 inch of oil in a small skillet until the oil ripples. With tongs, dunk each tortilla in the oil long enough for it to go limp, a matter of seconds. Don't let the tortilla turn crisp. Repeat with the remaining tortillas. Drain on paper towels. Slice tortillas in quarters.

3. Make 2 to 3 layers of the tortilla pieces, chicken, chile, both cheeses, onion, and soup mixture. Leave enough soup mixture to top the casserole generously, covering all of the tortilla triangles.

4. Bake for 25 to 30 minutes, until heated through and bubbly. Serve immediately.

Working ahead: The casserole can be assembled up to 8 hours ahead and refrigerated. Let it sit at room temperature for 15 to 30 minutes before baking.

Pork and Red Chile Tamales

One of the indigenous foods of the Americas, likely brought from central Mexico to New Mexico by early Spanish colonists, tamales take many forms in different places. This has been the typical New Mexico version for well over a century. Residents eat them year-round but really feast on them at Christmas, when they become as common at any gathering of people as biscochito cookies.

Makes 24 tamales of approximately 4 ounces each, about 12 main-dish servings

Filling	Dough
1½ pounds pork loin	6 cups masa harina
1 medium onion, chopped	2 teaspoons salt
2 cups water	1 teaspoon baking powder, optional
2 tablespoons vegetable oil	
2 garlic cloves, minced	2 cups lard, softened, or vegetable oil
1 tablespoon all-purpose flour	
½ cup ground dried mild to medium New Mexican red chile	4½ cups water, or more as needed
¾ teaspoon salt	
¼ teaspoon crumbled dried Mexican oregano or marjoram	red chile sauce (page 23 or 24), or other red chile sauce, optional, warmed
	shredded cheddar cheese, optional
half of a 6-ounce package of dried cornhusks	

For filling

1. Preheat the oven to 350° F.

2. Place the pork and the onion in a medium-size baking dish and cover with the water. Bake for approximately 1½ hours, or until the meat is cooked through and pulls apart easily. Remove the pork from the stock. Set the meat aside to cool for a few minutes and refrigerate the stock. When the pork has cooled enough to handle, shred it finely, either using two forks or in a food processor. Strain the stock, skimming any fat from the surface. If the stock doesn't measure 2 cups, add water to make 2 cups of liquid. Reserve the pork and the stock.

3. Warm the oil in a heavy skillet over medium heat and add the garlic and the pork. Sprinkle the flour over the mixture and stir constantly for about 1 minute as the flour begins to brown. Add the chile, the reserved stock, salt, and oregano (or marjoram). Continue cooking over medium heat for 20 to 25 minutes, or

A Christmas "Tamalada"

The easiest and most enjoyable way to make tamales is with your extended family or a group of friends. We participate in an annual December tamale-making party, or *tamalada*, at the home of Jodi Delaney, Craig Coffman, and their daughters, Eve and Claire. Their neighbors, Jenny and Aaron, who have participated in this tradition all of their lives, take care of ordering thirty pounds or so of prepared masa from Alicia's Tortilleria on Santa Fe's south side, brave the holiday line to pick it up, and get a vat of cornhusks, or *ojas*, soaking. They haul all of this next door to Jodi and Craig's in a big red wagon.

A collection of families brings a favorite filling or two, mostly savory, though usually at least one is a sweet, dessert-type mixture. Over cider, sangria, snacks, and warm conversation, hands dig in and fingers fly. Several hours of spooning, smoothing, folding, and wrapping result in mounds of husk-wrapped tamales. Everyone takes home an assortment of varieties. It's like a holiday cookie exchange but with a much deeper heritage. All of us leave well nourished, full of true holiday cheer, and toting a bulging bag of tamales. You won't regret giving it a try.

until most of the liquid has evaporated and the meat is quite tender and a bit moist. Watch carefully toward the end of the cooking time, stirring frequently to prevent burning. Remove from heat and reserve the mixture.

For cornhusks

1. In a deep bowl or baking pan, soak the cornhusks in hot water to cover. After 30 minutes the husks should be softened and pliable. Separate the husks and, if needed, rinse them under running water to wash away any grit or brown silks. Keep them covered with water until you are ready to use each one.

For dough

1. Mix together in a very large bowl the masa harina, salt, and optional baking powder (which can help lighten the dough). Using a sturdy spoon or powerful electric mixer with a dough hook, mix in the lard and then the water, working the dough until smooth. When well blended, the masa should have the consistency of a moist, somewhat sticky cookie dough. Add more water if needed for the preferred consistency. Keep the dough loosely covered while working.

Assembly

1. Use approximately equal amounts of masa and filling. To make 24 4-ounce tamales, use 2 tablespoons of masa and filling for each tamale.

2. Form the tamales one by one. Blot excess water off a cornhusk with a clean dish towel. Hold the husk flat on one hand, smooth side up. (You may, depending on the size of the cornhusks, need to overlap two husks to form one tamale. Spread the dough over the husks together, just as if they were one.) With a rubber spatula or large spoon, spread a thin layer of masa across the husk but not to the edges. Top with filling spread more thickly through the dough's center, stopping short of the dough's edges. Fold the two long sides of the husk into the center, which will wrap the dough around the filling. Make sure that the dough's edges meet to enclose all of the filling. Fold up the pointy end of the husk. If you wish, tamales can be tied across their centers with ¼-inch-wide strips of torn corn husk. Otherwise, secure the tamale by laying it folded side down. Repeat the procedure until all the filling and masa are used.

3. Place a vegetable steamer in the bottom of a large pot. Pour in water to the level of the steamer. Pack tamales loosely in crisscross directions or stand them on end. Allow enough space between them for the steam to rise effectively. Cover the pot and cook over simmering water for about 1 to 1¼ hours, until the masa is firm and no longer sticks to the cornhusks. Unwrap one tamale to check its consistency. If it is still doughy, rewrap it, return it to the pot, and continue steaming for a few more minutes.

4. Tamales should be eaten warm. The husks are usually left on when tamales are served unadorned, to be removed by each guest at the table before eating. Then chile sauce can be added by those who wish. To plate them with the sauce, remove the husks in the kitchen and arrange them on plates or a platter and top with sauce. When served this way, tamales often have cheese scattered over the top.

Working ahead: The masa is best made shortly before forming the tamales because it spoils easily, but the filling can be made a day or two ahead of when you plan to form the tamales. The filling freezes decently, too, in which case it can be made several weeks in advance. For quicker cooking the day you plan to eat them, steam tamales until just barely done, about an hour, wrap tightly, and refrigerate for up to two days. Then steam for just long enough to heat them through, about 10 minutes.

Variations: If you already have carne adovada on hand, or would prefer it as a filling, use it in place of the pork here. Make sure it is well cooked down so that it will shred apart easily as a filling. The farther east you go into New Mexico ranch country, the more likely beef will appear in tamales. Beef chuck can be prepared to use as a filling in the same way as the pork, though we would leave out the oregano (or marjoram) in this case. A pinch or two of cumin is a better—if sometimes controversial—match.

Green Chile Calabacitas Tamales

Vegetarian and other vegetable-based dishes have flourished in northern New Mexico since the 1960s. The presence of multiple back-to-the-land communes, followed by the founding of a large Sikh community in the Española area, stimulated much of the interest in meatless meals. The Sikhs even ran what was probably the first vegetarian restaurant in Santa Fe, the 1970s-era Golden Temple, in the location of Café Pasqual's today. According to Leona Medina-Tiede, owner for decades of Leona's Restaurante in the village of Chimayó, she began her business of making zucchini and green chile tamales because of interest from Sikhs in the area. Today, virtually all other commercial tamale-makers offer some form of vegetable filling, too, and home cooks create loads of creative adaptations. This version, modeled on Leona's, is our favorite of the ones we've tried.

Makes 24 medium tamales, enough for 8 to 12 main-dish servings

Filling

3 pounds summer squash, preferably a mix of varieties such as zucchini, yellow crookneck, and light green rounder squash called generically calabacita, grated

1 tablespoon salt, or more to taste

1 cup chopped roasted New Mexican green chile, fresh or thawed frozen

1 cup corn kernels, fresh or frozen

¼ cup minced onion

2 garlic cloves, minced

half of a 6-ounce package of dried cornhusks

Dough

6 cups masa harina

1 tablespoon salt

1 teaspoon baking powder, optional

1⅔ cups vegetable oil

5 cups water or a combination of water and chicken stock (if you're not cooking for vegetarians), or more as needed

6 ounces shredded mild cheddar cheese

green chile sauce (page 23 or 24), optional

For filling

1. Place the squash in a colander. Toss it with 1 tablespoon salt and drain for at least 20 minutes in a clean sink or over a bowl. Press down on the squash with your fingers to drain more of its accumulated liquid.

2. In a small saucepan over medium-low heat, simmer the green chile with any of its juices, the corn, onion, and garlic. Cook just until the mixture is dry. Stir the mixture into the squash. Add more salt if you wish.

For cornhusks

1. Soak the cornhusks for at least 30 minutes in hot water to cover. The husks will become soft and pliable. Separate the softened cornhusks and rinse them under warm running water to wash away any grit or brown silks. Keep them covered in water until you are ready to use each one.

For dough

1. Stir the masa harina, salt, and optional baking powder (which can help lighten the dough) together in a large bowl. Pour in the oil, working it into the masa harina with your fingertips. Add the water and mix with your fingers, a sturdy spoon, or powerful electric mixer with a dough hook. When well blended, the masa should have the consistency of a moist, slightly sticky cookie dough. Add more water if needed for the preferred consistency. Keep the dough loosely covered while working.

Assembly

1. To assemble the tamales, use approximately equal amounts of masa and filling. To make 24 4-ounce tamales, use 2 tablespoons of masa and filling for each tamale.

2. Form the tamales one by one. Blot excess water off a cornhusk with a clean dish towel. Hold the husk flat on one hand, smooth side up. (You may, depending on the size of the cornhusks, need to overlap two husks to form one tamale. Spread the dough over the husks together, just as if they were one.) With a rubber spatula or large spoon, spread a thin layer of masa across the husk, but not to the edges. Top with filling spread more thickly through the dough's center, stopping short of the dough's edges. Fold the two long sides of the husk into the center, which will wrap the dough around the filling. Make sure that the dough's edges meet to enclose all of the filling. Fold up the pointy end of the husk. If you wish, tamales can be tied across their centers with ¼-inch-wide strips of torn cornhusk. Otherwise, secure the tamale by laying it folded side down. Repeat the procedure until all the masa, filling, and cheese are used.

3. Place a vegetable steamer in the bottom of a large pot. Pour in water to the level of the steamer. Pack tamales loosely in crisscross directions or stand them on end. Allow enough space between them for the steam to rise effectively. Cover the pot and cook over simmering water for about 1 to 1¼ hours until the masa is firm and no longer sticks to the cornhusk. Unwrap one tamale to check its consistency. If it is still doughy, rewrap it, return it to the pot, and continue steaming a few more minutes.

4. The tamales should be eaten warm. Serve the tamales in their husks, to be removed by each guest before eating. The tamales are also good topped with green chile sauce, but the husks should be removed before adding the sauce.

Variations: Priscilla Hoback, a former owner of Maria's in Santa Fe, put together another inspired vegetarian tamale option in about the same period that Leona Medina-Tiede started marketing her vegetarian tamales. Priscilla made a filling mixture of piñon nuts, a little sautéed onion, and grated mild cheese, sometimes with some corn kernels or chopped green chile. Because of the delicacy of the flavors, Priscilla wanted to make the tamales with fresh masa, but there was little of it routinely available around town, so she ground up hominy to make her own style of fresh masa. Today, Santa Fe and most other communities have tortillerias and other businesses selling fresh masa (sometimes frozen). "*Masa preparada para tamales*" is ready to use, with lard and other flavoring mixed in. If you want to make the masa vegetarian, or just want more control of the flavorings, ask for "*masa para tamales*." In both cases, the masa will be ground more coarsely than for tortillas. To ready masa para tamales for assembly, in an electric mixer whip together 2 pounds of the fresh masa with ¾ cup of fat, which can be vegetable oil, shortening, lard, softened butter, or a combination; then add 2 to 3 teaspoons of salt and about 1 cup of water or stock to get the soft sticky texture desired.

TIP

How to Set Up a Tamale Assembly Line

• Clear off a table or other decent-size work space.

• Line up bowls of soaked cornhusks, dough, filling, and one or more large platters or bowls for the finished tamales.

• Have clean dish towels and paper towels handy. Use them to dry standing water from cornhusks before smearing the dough on the husks and for cleaning up spills as they occur.

• Assign jobs and act like you're a supervisor on a factory floor.

Bean Burritos

Unless it's purchased for take-out purposes at a food stand, a New Mexican burrito is usually a plated affair, covered in sauce and other toppings, to be eaten with a knife and fork. For emphasis, this might be called in local parlance *bañada*, or "smothered," or even "wet." Whole or refried beans have remained a popular filling in New Mexico for the simple dish, even as meat has supplanted this old staple in most of the Southwest. Unlike in nearby Arizona, where these are called "burros," New Mexicans consistently refer to them with the diminutive "-ito" suffix, though they are almost never petite.

Serves 6

Garnish

4 small tomatoes, preferably Romas or Italian plum, chopped

1 cup chopped crisp lettuce

4 scallions, sliced

2 tablespoons minced cilantro

1 tablespoon minced onion

salt

splash of vinegar

6 thin flour tortillas (page 138), preferably 7 to 8 inches in diameter

6 cups drained well-seasoned pinto beans, such as Frijoles de Olla (page 126) or refried beans (page 127), warmed

¼ cup minced onion

4 cups red chile sauce (page 23 or 24) or other mild red chile sauce

4 ounces (1 cup) shredded Colby, mild cheddar, Monterey Jack, or asadero cheese

For garnish
1. In a small bowl, combine the ingredients with just enough vinegar to moisten.

Assembly
1. Heat the broiler.

2. Take one tortilla and place it on a heatproof plate. Spoon a generous cupful of the beans down the center of the tortilla and top with a sprinkling of onion. Roll up the tortilla snugly around the filling, arranging seam-side down on the plate. Repeat with the remaining tortillas and beans.

3. Top the burritos with equal portions of the chile sauce and cheese. Melt the cheese under the broiler.

4. Spoon portions of garnish over each burrito and serve immediately.

Crispy Beef and Potato Tacos with Norteño Salsa

Pat Greathouse, a native New Mexican food journalist originally from Las Cruces, waxes eloquently and enthusiastically about this style of taco. Often dismissed because of the ground beef or its "adulteration" with potato, these can be one of the glories of southwestern cooking when prepared with care. The potato actually elevates the flavor and texture of the ground beef, as both Margarita C. de Baca and Fabiola Cabeza de Baca Gilbert recognized in recipes decades ago. Gilbert's taco directions from 1949 even featured the now common hard tortilla shell, which makes it one of the earliest published sources of the idea (perhaps the first, as claimed in one online encyclopedia article). These authors directly or indirectly influenced the owner and cook at La Cocina in Española, which Pat visited frequently for its similar tacos. When the proprietor, Mrs. Martinez, decided to take them off the menu, she took pity on Pat and told her how to make them. One of her secrets was Kitchen Bouquet, a bottled savory condiment that food stylists use today to make food a richer brown. You can substitute soy sauce or tamari if you wish. Pat added the cumin in a bow to another of her favorite restaurants, El Nopalito in her hometown. The tacos are topped with the style of salsa found in the mountainous north, where the short growing season for fresh tomatoes limited their use.

Serves 6 to 8

Norteño Salsa

14- to 15-ounce can crushed or diced tomatoes, with juice, "fire-roasted" if you wish

½ medium white onion, finely diced

1 garlic clove

½ teaspoon cider or white vinegar

1 teaspoon or more crushed New Mexican red chile pequin or other crushed hot red chile

salt

Filling

1 pound ground beef, preferably an 80/20 mix of lean to fat

1 yellow onion, chopped

1 large clove garlic, minced

3 medium potatoes, peeled and diced, about 2½ cups

2 tablespoons Kitchen Bouquet, soy sauce, or tamari

1 teaspoon salt, or more to taste

½ teaspoon ground cumin

water

Taco shells

vegetable oil for deep-frying

1½ dozen corn tortillas

grated mild cheddar

shredded lettuce

chopped tomato

As part of her job in 1939 she published an extension circular titled *Historic Cookery.* Ten years later this became the core of the recipe section in a full book, *The Good Life*, a tribute to rural Hispano traditions in New Mexico that featured dishes "I knew as a child in my grandmother's home." She wrote other articles and books, including stories about life on the family ranch in *We Fed Them Cactus* (1954), but above all else she is remembered as a trailblazing educator and a grand dame of New Mexico cooking.

For salsa

1. Combine tomatoes, onion, garlic, vinegar, and a small amount of chile in a blender and puree. Taste and add more chile as you wish for zip and salt to taste. Pour into a bowl and refrigerate until needed.

For filling

1. Heat a large skillet over medium-high heat. Add the beef and cook it until it is uniformly browned. Break up the meat as it cooks, adding the onion when the meat has lost its raw color. When the onion turns translucent and begins to brown, add the garlic, potatoes, Kitchen Bouquet, salt, cumin, and enough water to cover the potatoes and meat. Bring the mixture to a boil, then lower to a simmer and cook for about 10 minutes. If the potatoes aren't tender by the time the water cooks out, add a little more water.

2. When the potatoes are quite tender, begin letting the meat and potato mixture brown in the pan. It will begin to stick as it browns. Turn the mixture several times, scraping up the browned bits that stick to the pan, and breaking the mixture into small pieces. When the potatoes have broken up and the filling has lots of browned flavor, add more salt if you wish. Keep the filling warm.

For taco shells

1. Heat at least 1 inch of oil in a large skillet until the oil ripples. With tongs, dunk a tortilla in the oil long enough for it to go limp, a matter of seconds. Don't let the tortilla turn crisp. Repeat with the remaining tortillas and blot them, if you wish, with paper towels.

2. Fill a tortilla with about 2 tablespoons of filling, fold in half, and secure with a toothpick. Repeat with the remaining tortillas and filling.

3. Raise the temperature of the oil to 350° F. Fry the tacos, in batches, until lightly brown and crisp. Drain well.

Assembly

1. Remove toothpicks and garnish with cheese, lettuce, and tomato. Serve with salsa and enjoy right away.

Variations: You can make these with ground dark turkey instead of beef, frying the meat in 2 tablespoons of vegetable oil to begin. Either this or the beef filling can also be used for tostadas, flautas, or taquitos if you like.

Chicken Tacos

Rita Younis of Santa Fe recalls her mother, Angelina Delgado, now in her nineties, having to go to work to support herself and her four children after the early death of Rita's father. Meals out were not an option. To make each child feel special for his or her birthday, Angelina always let them pick the meal she would prepare for them to celebrate the day. Every year, Rita picked these chicken tacos, flavored with green olives and capers. Angelina liked mixing the Spanish ingredients into the filling to make it distinctive. Rita says it's okay to use store-bought taco shells, if you wish, to save the clean-up from frying your own shells, but we think it's worth the extra effort for maximum taste and texture. You don't even need salsa to enhance the flavor. Good cooking seems to be in this family's genes. Angelina's sister—and Rita's aunt and godmother—was Lucy Delgado, home cook, caterer, and author of the delightful *Comidas de New Mexico* (1979).

Serves 6

Filling

3½-ounce jar pimiento-stuffed
   green olives

1 tablespoon vegetable oil

1 medium onion, chopped fine

1 medium tomato, chopped

1 garlic clove, minced

4 cups cubed or shredded
   cooked chicken and any
   juices

1 heaping tablespoon small
   capers

1 teaspoon crumbled dried
   Mexican oregano or marjoram

1 teaspoon ground cumin

salt

Taco shells

vegetable oil for deep-frying

18 corn tortillas

shredded lettuce

guacamole (page 51)

store-bought hot sauce, such
   as North of the Border or
   Cholula

For filling

1. Drain off and reserve the juice from the olives. Chop the olives.

2. Warm 1 tablespoon of vegetable oil in a skillet over medium heat. Add the onion and cook several minutes until translucent. Stir in the tomato and garlic and cook briefly, until the tomato softens. Stir in the chicken, olives and olive juice, capers, oregano (or marjoram), and cumin. Taste before the salt goes in, since the olives, olive juice, and capers are all salty ingredients. The filling is ready when the liquid has evaporated. Keep warm.

For taco shells

1. Heat 1 inch of oil in a skillet until the oil ripples. With tongs, dunk a tortilla in the oil long enough for it to go limp, a matter of seconds. Repeat with the remaining tortillas and blot them, if you wish, with paper towels.

2. Fill a tortilla with about 2 tablespoons of filling, fold in half, and secure with a toothpick. Repeat with the remaining tortillas and filling.

3. Raise the temperature of the oil to 350° F. Fry the tacos, in batches, until lightly brown and crisp. Drain well.

Assembly

1. Remove toothpicks and garnish with lettuce and guacamole. Serve immediately, passing the hot sauce.

Indian Tacos

Not truly a taco in the ordinary sense of the term, this is more like a meaty salad scattered on top of a crunchy disk of fry bread. Depending on who is making the dish and where, it may be called a Navajo taco, Pueblo taco, or Tewa taco. We call it a real taste treat, though most street versions so ubiquitous at public festivals don't live up to the potential. For the best-tasting tacos, cook the fry bread after the filling is ready.

Serves 6

Filling

1 pound lean ground beef, bison, mutton, or lamb

½ teaspoon salt, or more to taste

1 medium onion, chopped

¾ to 1 cup chopped roasted New Mexican green chile, fresh or thawed frozen

2 cups cooked whole pinto beans, such as Frijoles de Olla (page 126), drained

Navajo fry bread (page 144)

about 2 cups shredded lettuce

8 ounces (2 cups) shredded mild cheddar cheese

2 medium tomatoes, diced

For filling

1. Warm a skillet over medium–high heat. Add the ground beef and ½ teaspoon salt. (Traditionally, most Diné and Pueblo dishes use very little salt.) Break up the meat with a spatula as it browns. When the meat has lost its raw color, add onion and continue to cook for several minutes, until the onion is translucent and soft.

2. Reduce heat to medium low, stir in the chile and beans and simmer for about 5 minutes. The filling should remain moist but not dripping with liquid. Add more salt if you wish. Keep warm.

Assembly

1. Spoon equal portions of filling on each fry bread to within about 1 inch of the bread's outside edge.

2. Scatter lettuce, cheese, and tomatoes equally over each taco and serve right away.

Chicken Flautas

These slim deep-fried "flutes" of tender chicken are similar to a crispy rolled taco or taquito, often known as a taquita in eastern New Mexico. Tacos, taquitos, and taquitas are usually seen as finger food, however, while flautas are more often served plated. You can make a poached-chicken filling for flautas by using the directions under Rolled Green Chile Chicken Enchiladas (page 76). However, since a somewhat drier filling works better in these we suggest using leftovers from a roast chicken or other chicken dinner. As common as leafy cilantro is in southwestern foods today, it was little used by traditional New Mexican cooks until the last few decades. It makes a nice addition here.

Serves 6

3 tablespoons whipping cream or half-and-half

1 garlic clove, minced

2 cups finely shredded cooked chicken

pinch of ground cumin

salt, optional

2 tablespoons minced cilantro, optional

18 thin corn tortillas

vegetable oil for deep-frying

salsa, such as Norteño Salsa (page 86) or Tomato Jalapeño Salsa (page 94)

guacamole (page 51)

sour cream or Mexican-style crema, optional

1. Warm the cream (or half-and-half) with the garlic in a saucepan over medium heat. Add the chicken and cumin and simmer until the cream is absorbed. Add salt if you wish. Stir in the optional cilantro.

2. Pour about 1½ inches of oil into a deep skillet or heavy saucepan. Heat the oil until it ripples. With a pair of tongs, briefly dip each tortilla into the hot oil. In a matter of a few seconds the tortilla will become limp. Remove it immediately and drain it. Repeat with the remaining tortillas.

3. Spoon 1½ to 2 tablespoons of filling on a tortilla and roll up tightly. Secure the flauta with a toothpick. Repeat with the remaining filling and tortillas.

4. Reheat the oil to 375° F. Add several flautas to the oil and fry for about 2 minutes until golden brown and crisp, turning as needed to cook evenly. Repeat with the remaining flautas. Remove the toothpicks and serve immediately, accompanied by salsa, guacamole, and the optional sour cream.

Variations: Making a turkey version of these with Thanksgiving leftovers is something of a tradition in our family. The Silver City Food Co-op recommended another variation using small fajita-size flour tortillas. The recipe called for filling the flautas with a late-summer mix of corn kernels, green chile, and grated Monterey Jack cheese before frying them in the same manner as the corn tortilla version here.

Tostadas Compuestas, Estila de La Posta

Katy Griggs Camuñez Meek founded what is probably the oldest continuously operating restaurant in the state, the famed La Posta de Mesilla, just a tortilla toss from Las Cruces. Katy learned to cook in her mother's kitchen and used mostly family recipes when she opened the doors in 1939. This dressed-up tostada, with the tortilla fried decoratively into a cup, was an exception, an invention of her own destined to become a classic in New Mexico. Elsewhere these would be called chalupas, with the tostada name reserved for a similar combination of ingredients served on a flat crisp tortilla. If you lack a tool in-house to form the tortilla cups, simply fry the tortillas flat until crisp, though you'll be missing a bit of Katy's flair.

Serves 4 to 6

Katy's Chile con Carne

2 tablespoons vegetable oil

1 pound pork loin in ½-inch cubes

1 tablespoon all-purpose flour

½ cup water

1 cup red chile sauce (page 23 or 24)

1 teaspoon ground cumin

½ teaspoon salt

½ teaspoon garlic salt

½ teaspoon crumbled dried Mexican oregano

12 corn tortillas

vegetable oil for deep-frying

2 cups refried beans (page 127) or other well-seasoned mashed cooked pinto beans, warmed

shredded lettuce

chopped tomatoes

shredded mild cheddar cheese

guacamole (page 51)

For chile con carne

1. Warm the oil in a large skillet over medium heat. Fry the pork in oil until brown. Add flour and mix well. Cook for another minute, then stir in the water and red chile sauce. Add the remaining ingredients. Reduce the heat to medium low and simmer until the pork is cooked through and tender, 15 to 25 minutes longer, depending on the meat.

Katy Griggs Camuñez Meek, 1920–1993

La Posta de Mesilla is memorable in most all ways, from the excellent New Mexican food to the storied restaurant premises. The building goes back to the earliest days of Mesilla, when settlers began moving there after the conclusion of the war with Mexico in 1848. The structure served as a major stop on the Butterfield Stage Line and later as the prestigious Corn Exchange Hotel. In these formative decades Mesilla was a bustling burg, the largest town on the stagecoach route between San Antonio, Texas, and San Diego, California.

Katy Griggs was even more remarkable than the historic edifice. In 1939, at the age of nineteen, she opened La Posta as a tiny "chile joint" in a corner of the building that her uncle sold her for "one dollar, love and affection." With her mother cooking at the back of the room and just four tables on the dirt floor, Katy presided as an ebullient hostess, greeting guests, taking orders, making tongue-in-cheek risqué remarks, and charming everyone. In slower moments she snuck out the back door and took fresh food to neighbors in need.

La Posta has grown enormously over time in space and fame, but the menu has stayed basically the same. Katy gave out most of the recipes in her *La Posta Cook Book* (1971), which remains the guiding beacon for the current owners-managers, Katy's grandniece Jerean Camuñez Hutchinson and her husband, Tom. As the restaurant celebrated its seventieth anniversary in 2009, it had clearly proved its claim to be still everyone's favorite stop on the old Butterfield Stage Line.

For tostada shells

1. You will need some kind of round but flat-ended tool, perhaps a wooden flour tortilla roller or a cylindrical bean or potato masher. Pour enough oil into a deep heavy skillet to measure at least 3 inches in depth. Heat the oil to 375° F. While the oil is warming, cut 4 evenly spaced 1½-inch deep slits toward the center of each tortilla.

2. Place the first tortilla in oil and immediately press down on it with your chosen device. The hot oil will force the tortilla back up toward your tool, forming a cup. Hold a slotted spoon in your other hand to help mold the cup shape uniformly as the tortilla crisps and colors lightly, 20 to 30 seconds. Remove the tortilla cup with the slotted spoon and drain it on a wire rack over paper towels. Repeat with the remaining tortillas.

Assembly

1. Spoon 2 heaping tablespoons of beans into each tortilla cup, followed by about 1½ tablespoons of carne con chile. Top generously with garnishes. Serve right away. Eat with a combination of fork and fingers.

Working ahead: Chile con carne is great made ahead a day or two and stored in the refrigerator. The beans also can be prepared a day ahead. Reheat both just before serving. Tostada shells can be made up to an hour before serving. Garnishes can all be prepared an hour or so ahead as well.

Gorditas

These "little fat ones" from southern New Mexico are deep-fried masa pockets, overflowing with meat, beans, and toppings. As good as they are, it's surprising they haven't spread more widely north of Hatch. Similar dishes from Mexico may have inspired them originally, though the chile flavoring gives them a distinctive New Mexico touch. Emma Jean Cervantes, who has lived most of her life in the Mesilla Valley, speculates that the popularity of gorditas in her area sprang from their functionality as a sturdy all-in-one meal for farmworkers to take to the fields. The masa envelope would hold the filling without getting too soggy by midday. Often workers would build a small communal fire and heat a number of gorditas on a griddle or grill placed over it. Other common fillings include chile con carne (page 54), prepared with either green or red chile, and beans with guacamole. You can make the common local-style salsa for the gorditas, too, or serve them with any other favorite version.

Makes 8 5- to 6-inch gorditas, enough for 4 main-dish servings

Tomato Jalapeño Salsa

4 to 8 fresh jalapeño chiles

1½ cups chopped tomatoes, fresh or drained diced canned

¼ teaspoon vinegar

½ teaspoon salt or garlic salt, or more to taste

Ground Beef Filling

2 tablespoons vegetable oil

1 medium onion, minced

4 garlic cloves, minced

2 pounds freshly ground beef chuck

1 medium russet potato, parboiled, peeled, and diced fine

1 tablespoon all-purpose flour

½ teaspoon salt, or more to taste

½ teaspoon crumbled dried Mexican oregano or marjoram, optional

¾ teaspoon ground dried New Mexican red chile

¾ cup beef stock, chicken stock, or water

Dough

2 cups masa harina

⅓ cup all-purpose flour

1 teaspoon salt

1 teaspoon baking powder

3 tablespoons vegetable oil or vegetable shortening

1⅓ cups warm water, or more as needed

vegetable oil for deep-frying

¾ cup refried beans (page 127) or other well-seasoned mashed cooked pinto beans, warmed, optional

shredded lettuce

shredded mild cheddar or Monterey Jack cheese

For salsa

1. Place the jalapeños in a small saucepan and cover with water by 1 or 2 inches over high heat and bring to a boil. Reduce the heat and simmer for about 10 minutes. Drain and when cool enough to handle slice away stems and seeds. Wear rubber gloves to handle the chiles. Mince 1 jalapeño and reserve.

2. Transfer the rest of the jalapeños to a food processor and add the tomatoes, vinegar, and salt. Pulse until mostly smooth. Stir in the minced jalapeño. Refrigerate until ready to serve.

For filling

1. Warm the oil in a heavy skillet over medium heat. Stir in the onion and garlic and sauté for a couple of minutes until softened. Add the meat and fry until it has lost all pink color. Stir in the potato, flour, salt, oregano, and chile. Pour in the stock (or water). Reduce the heat to low and simmer for another 10 minutes or until the potato bits are very soft and most of the liquid has evaporated.

For dough

1. Combine the masa harina, flour, salt, and baking powder in a food processor. Add the oil (or shortening) and process just until mealy. Pour in the water and process until the dough becomes smooth and moist. Add a little more water, if needed, for the desired consistency. Take the dough out of the processor, form it into a ball, and cover it in plastic wrap. Let the dough sit for at least 20 minutes and up to 1 hour.

2. Divide the dough into 8 balls and flatten each to about ½-inch thickness, rounding rough edges. Cover the dough rounds loosely with plastic wrap.

3. In a Dutch oven or large heavy saucepan, heat 3 to 4 inches of oil to 365° F. Fry the dough rounds in batches, cooking them for 4 to 5 minutes until golden and crisp. Turn them or hold them under the oil with tongs for even cooking. Drain and repeat with the remaining dough.

Assembly

1. Slice a gordita open on the edge, cutting about ⅓ of the way around it. With your fingers or a spoon, scrape out any uncooked dough from the center, leaving a hollow. Repeat with the remaining gorditas.

2. If using the beans, coat the insides of the gorditas with a generous tablespoon in each, and then spoon in the ground beef mixture to fill the gorditas about ⅔ full. Top with lettuce and cheese, and serve immediately, accompanied by salsa.

Working ahead: The salsa can be made early in the day you plan to serve it. The ground beef filling can be made a day ahead. Dough can be formed and kept covered for an hour before frying. Once fried, the gordita shells can be kept warm in a single layer on a baking sheet in a 200° F oven for about 1 hour.

Chiles Rellenos, Southern Style

New Mexico boasts two distinct styles of chiles rellenos. An occasional visitor probably wouldn't notice the difference—it mostly boils down to the batter—but in the state it can get contentious, like a disagreement over authentic clam chowder between cooks in Massachusetts and Manhattan. Our model for this fabulous version comes from the kitchens of the Benevidez sisters at Chope's in La Mesa and the Hernandez family at Nellie's Café in Las Cruces. The rellenos resemble some from south of the border, with a tender, eggy batter coating that almost dissolves on your tongue. Unlike Mexican rellenos, though, these are typically covered in gooey cheese and the local green chile sauce. They're worth every calorie and minute of preparation and clean-up.

Serves 6 or more

12 whole roasted and peeled large New Mexican green chiles, slit from end to end

12 ounces (about 3 cups) shredded cheese, preferably Monterey jack, muenster, or asadero

vegetable oil or shortening for deep-frying

1 cup all-purpose flour

green chile sauce (page 26), warmed

Batter

6 large eggs, separated

½ cup all-purpose flour

¾ teaspoon salt

1. With your fingers, stuff each chile with cheese, filling them well but not to overflowing.

2. Preheat oven to 400° F.

For batter

1. Beat the egg whites in a large bowl with an electric mixer until soft peaks form. Mix in egg yolks, ½ cup flour, and salt, beating only until combined. The batter should be lightly stiff and thick enough to coat the chiles.

Assembly

1. Heat 4 inches of oil in a large heavy pan to 350° F. Place a baking rack over a few thicknesses of paper towels within easy reach of the stovetop.

Big Jim

Chile farming in the southern part of the state didn't start booming until the 1960s and '70s. The 1975 release of the "NuMex Big Jim," designed to be a large chile perfect for rellenos, helped to stimulate the emerging crop specialty and brought national attention to the area.

Professor Roy Nakayama at NMSU worked closely with June and Jim Lytle, early chile farmers, in testing the cultivation of the new pod, which earned June a spot in the *Guinness Book of World Records* for growing a 13½-inch chile, the longest on record. The Lytles also pioneered mechanical dehydration of chiles, another major booster for the industry.

Jim died in 1970, but Nakayama helped to preserve his memory by naming his famous chile after its first farmer. Jim Lytle Jr. and his son Faron carry on the family farming tradition today and ship pods of all sizes to chile lovers nationwide through their Hatch Chile Express (www.hatch-chile.com, 505-267-3226).

2. Pour 1 cup of flour onto a plate.

3. Lay the first chile, seam-side up, in the flour to coat, using a spoon to cover it thoroughly. Dunk the chile into the batter, again seam-side up, and spoon more batter over it. When evenly coated, pull it from the batter by its stem and let any excess batter drip back into the bowl. No cheese should show—the batter should be thick enough to seal the chile's seam. Slip the chile into the oil and repeat with the remaining chiles as you have room in the pan.

4. Fry the chiles for about 4 to 5 minutes, turning as needed to fry them until evenly golden and crisp. Drain the chiles on the baking rack.

5. Transfer the chiles to a heatproof platter or individual plates, then top with chile sauce and cheese. Pop in the oven for about 3 minutes, until the cheese on top has melted. Serve immediately.

Variations: At the Hatch Chile Festival, the annual Labor Day weekend celebration, vendors leave out the sauce and wrap the rellenos in flour tortillas to make them finger food. Sometimes a smear of refried beans helps to keep the tortilla closed. According to a vintage issue of *New Mexico* magazine, Roy Nakayama, the New Mexico State University chile breeder who developed the "NuMex Big Jim" chile, recommended a Japanese-style tempura batter for rellenos. If you want to try that idea, take a look at the recipe for Green Chile Tempura (page 122). Another Asian influence slipped into the dish in *Simply Simpatico* (1981), the Junior League of Albuquerque's wildly successful cookbook. The ladies suggested using egg-roll wrappers, rather than batter, to envelope the chiles, an unconventional idea that tastes remarkably good. Moisten the edges of the wrapper with water to secure, then fry them at a slightly lower temperature of 325° F.

Chiles Rellenos, Northern Style

Most of the heirloom chiles raised in the north are too small, wrinkly, and thin-walled to be good for stuffing, so cooks in the area frequently use green chiles from the south or genetically "improved" breeds of local pods. The batter is commonly thicker and crunchier than the southern counterpart and sometimes includes the cornmeal we use here. The effervescence of beer or club soda helps lighten the mixture. For the cheese filling, some cooks simply slip in rectangular slices of cheese, which is neater than working with a pile of shredded cheese. However, the shredded variety melts more readily and evenly, and allows you to mix in a little of a dried herb to cut the richness of the cheese.

Serves 6

8 ounces (about 2 cups) shredded Monterey Jack cheese

4 ounces (about 1 cup) shredded Colby or mild cheddar cheese

2 teaspoons dried Mexican oregano, marjoram, or epazote, optional

12 whole roasted and peeled medium to large New Mexican green chiles, slit from end to end

Batter

4 large eggs

approximately ¾ cup beer or club soda

1¼ cups all-purpose flour

2 tablespoons yellow or white cornmeal

¾ teaspoon salt

vegetable oil for deep-frying

green chile sauce (page 26), or other green chile sauce, warmed

For filling

1. In a bowl, combine the cheeses with the optional oregano (or marjoram or epazote). With your fingers, stuff each chile with cheese, filling them full but not to overflowing.

For batter

1. Separate 2 of the eggs, placing egg whites in the bowl of an electric mixer. Beat until soft peaks form.

2. In a large bowl, combine the 2 egg yolks, 2 eggs, ¾ cup beer (or club soda), flour, cornmeal, and salt. The batter should seem pourable but thick enough to coat the chiles. If too thick, add more beer.

Assembly

1. Heat 4 inches of oil in a large heavy pan to 350° F. Place a baking rack over a few thicknesses of paper towels within easy reach of the stovetop.

2. Lay the first chile in the batter, seam-side up and spoon more batter over it. When evenly coated, pull it from the batter by its stem and let any excess batter drip back into the bowl. No cheese should show—the batter should be thick enough to seal the chile's seam. Slip the chile into the oil and repeat with remaining chiles, as you have room in the pan.

3. Fry the chiles for about 4 to 5 minutes, turning as needed to fry them evenly until golden and crispy. Drain the chiles on the baking rack.

4. Transfer the chiles to a platter or individual plates and top with green chile sauce. Alternatively, spoon the sauce onto the plates and arrange the chiles over it. Serve immediately.

Variations: We tend to prefer chiles rellenos served with the complementary flavor of green chile sauce, but plenty of diners choose red for contrast, particularly when the filling is meat instead of cheese. Also popular is a ranchero-style sauce with tomatoes, onions, and some chile. Choose what you like best. For meaty rellenos, most cooks fill the chile with a ground beef mixture like one often used in tacos.

Stuffed Sopaipillas

Sopaipillas—sometimes spelled sopapillas —are fried poofs of flour dough, which hollow naturally as they inflate in hot oil. On their own, they accompany meals as bread in the north, and in the south they serve as a dessert. In both instances, the dough often includes sugar. In this instance, though, a savory version becomes a key player in a popular main dish. We love these positively bulging with carne adovada, but chile con carne (made with beef, pork, or lamb), refried beans, or even calabacitas are other good stuffing options.

Makes 12 sopaipillas, enough for 6 main-dish servings

Savory Sopaipillas

2 cups all-purpose flour

1 teaspoon salt

1 teaspoon baking powder

1½ teaspoons vegetable oil or vegetable shortening

¼ cup milk, at room temperature

approximately ½ cup lukewarm water

vegetable oil for deep-frying

½ recipe Carne Adovada (page 55), warmed

onion or tomato, or both, chopped

lettuce, sliced thin

For sopaipillas

1. In a large mixing bowl, stir together the flour, salt, and baking powder. Mix in the oil with your fingertips. Add the milk and water, working the liquids into the flour until a sticky dough forms. Add a bit more water if necessary.

2. Lightly dust a counter or pastry board with flour and knead the dough vigorously for 1 minute. In texture, the mixture should feel like your earlobe, soft but with a bit of resistance at its core, and no longer sticky. Let the dough rest, covered with a damp cloth, for 15 minutes. Divide the dough into 3 balls, cover the balls with the damp cloth, and let them rest for another 15 to 30 minutes. (The dough can be refrigerated at this point for up to 4 hours.)

Where One May Dig or Dream

I say no more of New Mexico as it is today, except that here surely is a place where many kinds of men live and work, where one may dig or dream, make poems, bricks or love, or merely sit in the sun, and find some tolerance and some companionship. Here handicraft as well as the machine has some place in life, the primitive persists beside the civilized, the changeless mountains offer refuge to the weary sons of change.
—HARVEY FERGUSSON, *RIO GRANDE* (1955)

3. Lightly dust a counter or pastry board with flour again and roll out each ball of dough into a circle or oval approximately ¼-inch thick. If you have a tortilla roller, use it rather than a heavier rolling pin, which compacts the dough more. Trim off any ragged edges and discard them. To avoid toughening the dough, try to avoid rerolling it. Cut each circle of dough into 4 wedges.

4. In a heavy high-sided saucepan or skillet, heat the oil to 400° F. Carefully transfer 1 or 2 wedges of dough to the oil. After sinking briefly, the sopaipillas should begin to balloon and rise back to the surface. Spoon some oil over the top of the sopaipillas as they cook. When the top surfaces are fully puffed, a matter of seconds, turn the sopaipillas. Cook just until the sopaipillas are light golden and then drain them. While warm, slice open an end of each sopaipilla with kitchen scissors, creating an airy pouch.

Assembly

1. Spoon about ½ cup carne adovada into each sopaipilla. Arrange 2 per serving. Scatter each with onion, tomato, lettuce, or other toppings and serve right away.

Variations: Use whole pintos, refried beans, or shredded chicken or beef as a filling. Place on a heatproof platter or plates. Top with a good ladle of red or green chile and about 2 tablespoons of shredded cheese per sopaipilla and broil just until cheese melts.

6 Chicken, Lean Meats, and Fish

The Puebloans have often relied for sustenance on game animals and fish, and the Spanish settlers in New Mexico were adept hunters as well, used to supplementing their domesticated meat supplies with wild species. What both groups took from the land and streams was naturally lean, like the chickens introduced by the Spanish, and often too delicate or spare for the robust chile preparations used on heartier meats.

Trout abound in New Mexico rivers and lakes, particularly ones fed by cool mountain waters, and they have long been the most popular fish in the state for anglers and eaters alike. Other lake fish such as bass also flourish but have never challenged trout for supremacy on the plate. Although New Mexicans have imported live oysters and dried shrimp for a couple of centuries, and other seafood in more recent periods, our cooks have never developed special preparations for any saltwater favorites.

Among the many game animals found nearby, deer, elk, and bison were the most cherished for their meat. New Mexicans also hunted smaller creatures such as rabbits and birds, but they provided much less food relative to effort and the fare never really attained an elevated status on the table. Despite the fondness for venison and bison, few historic game dishes have survived the test of time, so our recipes feature cuts and seasoning styles of recent decades.

Pollo con Arroz

Spaniards spread the love of rice-and-chicken preparations around the Americas, but the one that evolved in New Mexico is more austere than the vegetable-enriched pollo con arroz common in more verdant areas such as Cuba and Puerto Rico. Whether the pollo or the arroz came first in the name of local versions seems to have depended on the cook and perhaps small differences in the manner of preparation. What never varied was the soothing and simple nature of the dish, which is definitely worth the search for a superior bird.

Serves 6 or more

2 tablespoons olive oil

3½- to 4-pound chicken, cut into 8 pieces

1 small onion, minced

2 garlic cloves, sliced thin

6 cups water

1½ teaspoons salt

1 teaspoon New Mexican azafrán or 1 pinch saffron threads, optional

1½ cups raw long-grain rice

fresh mint leaves, minced, optional

1. Warm the oil over medium-high heat in a Dutch oven or other large heavy pot. Brown the skin of each piece of chicken, in batches if necessary. When the pieces have lost their raw color dump the onion and garlic over the chicken. Add the water, salt, and optional azafrán or saffron. Bring to a boil over high heat. Skim off and discard any accumulating foam. Reduce the heat to a bare simmer, cover, and poach the chicken until cooked through, about 25 minutes.

2. Add the rice and cover the pot again, cooking for 18 to 20 minutes more. Remove the pot from the heat. Set it aside without opening, to steam the rice for 10 minutes. The mixture should remain somewhat soupy.

3. Spoon rice and juices on a platter with chicken pieces on top. Sprinkle with optional mint and serve.

Variations: The Atencio family from Española, who own El Paragua and several El Parasols in northern New Mexico, still prepare the dish as family matriarch Frances made it for them at home. It's full of poultry goodness but contains cubed bits of chicken rather than bone-in pieces. To simulate this, bone and cube the chicken after poaching and return the meat to the pot with the rice.

Pollo Real

One way to ensure getting a superior chicken for pollo con arroz is to shop for a plump local bird, such as those that Tom and Tracey Delehanty raise on their Socorro acreage, the first certified organic poultry farm in the country. In business almost twenty years now, the couple sells their Pollo Real chickens to some of the finest restaurants in the state, at the Santa Fe Farmers' Market, and in select co-op stores. Tom and Tracey developed their own grazing system for their beloved birds. They move the chickens daily in portable pens through fields planted with chicory, millet, wheatgrass, and brassicas, and supplement the free-range diet with other grains. They use no pesticides, hormones, antibiotics, growth enhancers, or meat by-products, and to eliminate the stress and injuries caused by long-distance hauling, they hand process the chickens in a USDA-inspected facility on their own farm.

Jesusita Romero with her goats. She was the local lechera, the woman who made queso fresco and requesón (ricotta) from her goat's milk. Chacón, NM, 1995.

Compadres (from left) Arturo Lujan, Max Bernal, Eduardo Trujillo, and Tony Olivas take a break after slaughtering a pig in the matanza tradition of Northern New Mexico, Chacón, NM, 1998.

Macario Torrez's field irrigated by acequia waters in El Cerrito, NM, 2005.

Baked Chicken Piñon

Albuquerque resident Millie Santillanes was a fabulous home cook who contributed pages of recipes to *La Herencia* magazine's tenth anniversary cookbook, *Las Comidas de los Abuelos* (2005). Born in Old Town into the Duran y Chavéz family who helped to found the Villa de San Felipe de Albuquerque in 1706, she was a tireless promoter of her hometown and New Mexico Hispano culture. She passed away in 2007, but her many civic accomplishments live on, as will her recipes, from which this dish derives.

Serves 6

¾ cup buttermilk

1 medium egg

1 cup all-purpose flour

1 teaspoon salt

½ teaspoon freshly milled black pepper

½ teaspoon sweet paprika

¾ cup finely chopped piñon nuts

6 boneless skinless individual chicken breasts, about 6 ounces each

6 tablespoons unsalted butter, melted

3 tablespoons whole piñon nuts

1. Preheat oven to 375° F. Grease a 9 by 13 baking dish.

2. Whisk together in a shallow dish the buttermilk and egg. On a plate combine the flour, salt, pepper, paprika, and chopped piñon nuts.

3. Dunk the first chicken breast in the buttermilk mixture and then in the flour mixture. Place it in the baking dish. Repeat with the remaining chicken.

4. Drizzle chicken breasts equally with melted butter. Scatter the whole piñon nuts over the chicken.

5. Bake the chicken uncovered for about 30 minutes, until it is golden brown with an opaque white center. You can check the internal temperature, too, which should be about 170° F, by inserting an instant-read thermometer into a chicken breast horizontally. Serve the chicken hot, cut across the grain into thin slices if you wish.

A Tribute to Local Birds

New Mexico's first cookbook author after statehood also liked the combination of chicken and piñon nuts. In the introduction to a chicken recipe in *The Original New Mexico Cookery* (1916), Alice Stevens Tipton told her readers, "Select for the foundation of this dish one of New Mexico's large fowls, preferably one that has been raised in the open and fed on piñon nuts. This state raises the best poultry that the markets afford, and the climatic conditions insure absolutely healthy fowls at all seasons of the year."

Slow-Roasted Cabrito

When New Mexicans ate goat in the past, it was usually mature animals beyond further usefulness. With care in preparation, this meat can be tasty, but it pales in comparison to cabrito, or milk-fed kid, a special New Mexico treat frequently enjoyed at Easter or on other festive occasions. Often cooks slow-roast a whole kid in hornos, the beehive-shaped outdoor ovens seen around northern New Mexico, but for a standard kitchen oven a hindquarter is more manageable. For a good fit, even that cut should be sliced into two shorter sections by your butcher or at home with a cleaver. Avoid the slimmer, bonier forequarters, best stewed and shredded for tacos or other dishes.

Serves 6 to 8

Marinade

2 12-ounce bottles or cans of beer

½ cup vinegar, cider or white

1 medium onion, chopped

1 head of garlic, cut in half crosswise

2 tablespoons ground dried mild to medium-hot New Mexican red chiles

2 tablespoons vegetable oil

1 tablespoon salt

1 cabrito hindquarter (haunch and leg), 4 to 5 pounds, bone-in, halved into 2 shorter portions

6 tablespoons unsalted butter

1 bunch of mint, minced

1. At least 4 hours and up to the night before you plan to roast the cabrito, make enough refrigerator space for the hindquarter to marinate overnight in a roasting pan or large (2-gallon) food-safe plastic bag. Place the hindquarter sections in the pan or bag. Combine the marinade ingredients and pour over the meat. Stash the bundle overnight in the fridge.

2. Remove all but the lowest baking rack from the oven. Preheat the oven to 300° F.

3. Drain the marinade from the cabrito, saving half of it and most of the onion. Place the 2 portions of cabrito side by side on a rack in a roasting pan. Pour the saved marinade back over the meat, with most of the onion on top of the meat.

4. Plan on a cooking time of about 2½ hours. While the meat cooks, combine the butter and mint in a small saucepan and melt over low heat. After 30 minutes, brush the top sides of the cabrito with the butter mixture. Repeat every 30 minutes. Check to make sure there is still liquid in the bottom of the pan. If it is nearly dry, pour in a few tablespoons of water, just enough to create some steam. If you run out of the butter mixture, spoon out some of the pan drippings and brush the meat with that.

5. Let the cabrito sit at room temperature for about 15 minutes, until cool enough to handle. Pull large chunks of the meat off the bones, discarding fat, cartilage, and bone. Slice the meat across the grain and serve warm, with the pan drippings if you wish.

Variations: The founding chef–owner of Santa Fe's Coyote Café, Mark Miller, taught us how to emulate the slow-roasted character of a horno oven by baking in clay. For a cabrito hindquarter, you need a good 10 pounds of nontoxic terra-cotta clay (available from Ceramic King in Albuquerque, 800-781-2529 or 505-881-2350). Roll the clay out into a ½-inch-thick rectangle, then cover the clay with a piece of foil of the same size. Make sure the cabrito will fit into your oven! In the largest pan you can find, sear the hindquarter as best you can on all sides. Let cool. Place a bed of fresh mint (or sage or rosemary) on the foil. Arrange the meat over the foil. Scatter garlic slivers over the cabrito and herbs. Fold the foil up around the cabrito, leaving the last few inches of the leg bone exposed. Crimp it tightly. Fold the clay up over the foil and seal it tightly. Place the cabrito on a parchment-covered baking sheet. Bake in a 225° F oven for about 4 hours. Let the meat sit about 15 minutes at room temperature. Crack the clay open with a kitchen mallet. The clay will pull away from the foil wrapping and can then be discarded or returned to the earth to naturally break down in soil. Unwrap and serve.

Bison Steaks

Before their systematic slaughter in the nineteenth century, bison roamed in vast herds through the grasslands of the Great Plains, close enough to New Mexico's early population centers for Pueblo and Hispano hunters to pursue them as game. By the time of statehood, the number of surviving bison had dwindled from the millions to the hundreds, but they are making a comeback today. Some high-profile New Mexico ranch owners—Ted Turner and Val Kilmer, in particular—raise bison, and so do an increasing number of Pueblo villages, some of which sell meat at farmers' markets. Treat yourself to a rib eye or other serious steak when you get the opportunity.

Serves 2 or more

Steaks

2 teaspoons coarse salt, such as kosher or sea salt

2 teaspoons freshly ground black pepper

1 teaspoon dried crumbled Mexican oregano or marjoram

1 teaspoon cornstarch

2 1-inch-thick bison rib eye or strip steaks, 12 to 14 ounces each

Worcestershire Butter (optional)

¼ cup melted unsalted butter

2 teaspoons Worcestershire sauce

vegetable oil spray

For steaks

1. Stir together the salt, pepper, oregano, and cornstarch (which helps form a crust). Rub the mixture generously over all surfaces of the steaks. Let sit covered at room temperature for about 30 minutes.

For optional Worcestershire butter

1. Stir Worcestershire sauce into melted butter and keep warm.

Assembly

1. See How to Grill Like a Pro (page 66. Fire up a grill to cook over high heat (1 to 2 seconds with the hand test).

2. Spray steaks lightly on both sides with oil.

Los Ciboleros

New Mexicans obtained most of their bison meat and hides in trade with Plains Indians, but even before the arrival of the Spanish, Puebloans also mounted hunting expeditions to the high plains of eastern New Mexico and the Texas panhandle. Early Spanish settlers, who called the bison *cibolos*, started doing the same in the seventeenth century, and these *ciboleros* continued the pursuit of the animals for around two hundred years.

The hunts usually took place in October, shortly after farm harvests, and sometimes involved as many as 150 people. Riding on horseback, the *ciboleros* used bows and arrows as weapons, or more commonly razor-sharp spears, and a skilled hunter could down as many as twenty-five bison during a single chase of two or three miles. Even while the lancers worked, other men in the party began skinning fallen animals and loading the meat onto horses or carts to be carried to their campsite, where they cut it into thin slices to dry as jerky.

3. Plan to grill the steaks for a total of 8 to 10 minutes with each side facing the fire twice. (Avoid cooking lean bison steaks beyond medium-rare.) Grill the steaks over high heat for about 2 minutes per side. Rotate a half-turn when you flip the steaks the final two times, for crisscross grill marks. (If juices begin to pool on the surface, give the steaks an extra turn.)

4. For 2 hearty eaters, arrange steaks on plates and top each with half of the butter. If serving more diners, let steaks sit for 5 minutes, then slice across the grain about ½-inch thick and arrange on plates with any juices. Drizzle with butter and serve right away.

Variations: The steaks can be pan-seared instead of grilled. You need a serious cast-iron skillet or griddle for worthy results. Heat the dry skillet over high heat for about 5 minutes before beginning to cook. Spray the steaks with oil just before you place them in the skillet. The timing will be about the same as for the grilled steak. Any dried spice rub mixture you use for beef steaks can be good on bison. Just don't add too many disparate flavors to the lean but dense meat.

Roasted Venison Backstrap

From the San Juans near Chama in the north to the Gila and Cibola wilderness and forest areas of the south, elk, mule or whitetail deer, and pronghorn antelope roam freely and attract plenty of hunters, some of whom still stalk game with only a bow and arrows. Cooks cube or grind much of the venison for dishes such as *temole* or other types of chile stew or as a filling for tamales. They almost always reserve the backstrap, or tenderloin, however, for special treatment. Here we pair it with chokecherries, known as *capulin* regionally, which ripen in the late summer. Some families continue to harvest buckets of chokecherries in the wild, but many folks grow them today, too. Substitute sour-cherry puree or juice instead if you wish.

Serves 6

4 garlic cloves

2 teaspoons fresh rosemary leaves or 1 teaspoon dried rosemary leaves

2 teaspoons salt

2 teaspoons freshly ground black pepper

3 teaspoons vegetable oil (divided use)

2 ¾-pound venison backstrap (loin) sections

1 tablespoon unsalted butter

¼ cup dry red wine

2 cups pureed pitted chokecherries or sour cherries or sour cherry juice

1 small chipotle chile from a can of chipotles in adobo, minced

pinch or 2 brown sugar, optional

1. Using a mortar and pestle, make a paste of the garlic, rosemary, salt, pepper, and 1 teaspoon oil. Smear the paste over all surfaces of the venison. Cover the meat and let it sit 20 minutes at room temperature. Preheat the oven to 425° F.

2. Heat a large cast-iron skillet over high heat. When very hot, add 2 teaspoons of oil and swirl around to coat the skillet evenly. Sear backstrap sections, browning all surfaces, including the ends, about 1 minute per side.

3. Place the skillet with venison in the oven and roast for 15 to 18 minutes, until the meat registers 125° F to 130° F on an instant-read thermometer inserted into the thickest portion of one of the backstraps. Expect some smoke in the oven. Remove meat to a cutting board and tent with foil.

4. If any of the spice mixture has scorched badly in the skillet, spoon it out. Otherwise, place the still-hot skillet back on the stovetop and melt the butter into any pan drippings (there will not be much). Turn on the heat to medium high and pour in the wine. Reduce the wine by about half, then stir in the chokecherry puree and chipotle chile and cook down by about ⅓. Adjust seasoning in the sauce with more salt or pepper and if too tart mix in a bit of brown sugar.

5. Cut the venison across the grain into thin slices. Plate with sauce over or under the meat and enjoy right away.

The Powdrell Family of Albuquerque

Pete and Catherine Powdrell migrated from Louisiana to Texas and on to New Mexico, arriving in Albuquerque in 1958 with their eleven children. One of the sons, Joe, who was born in West Texas, remembers the family living in Odessa in the 1940s in a partitioned tent divided into a home on one side and a barbecue restaurant on the other side. Joe says his parents "always had barbecue places. My dad's grandfather had given him a recipe for sauce and barbecue, and he used that."

In Albuquerque the family originally settled in the South Valley in an area populated primarily by other southern blacks and Hispanos of modest means. They shared a small house at first with folks from Mississippi who helped newcomers get established.

Within a few years Pete opened Mr. Powdrell's Barbeque House, which has become a food-lover's institution in the city. He and the other cooks borrowed ideas from all the barbecue capitals—Kansas City and Memphis, Texas and the Carolinas—and developed a style of their own with a distinctive southwestern sensibility. Of the many great restaurant success stories in New Mexico, the house that Pete built is among the best.

Fried Trout

One time, for an important dinner, we hoped to serve locally caught trout, despite our lack of angling skills. Cheryl stopped in our favorite market to ask advice from Santa Fe master butcher Art Pacheco, a wizard at sourcing meat, fowl, and fish. He demonstrated the true meaning of service by volunteering to go fishing himself. Cheryl wouldn't let him do that, though she did gratefully accept fresh trout from our electrician. Like in many other places frying is the most common way to prepare the fish in New Mexico, but here the cornmeal coating may be blue and there may be a light dusting of red chile. An Española community cookbook from 1965 offers the good suggestion of serving the fish with watermelon-rind pickles.

Serves 4

8 slices bacon, chopped

vegetable oil

4 trout, about ¾ to 1 pound each, gutted but heads intact

¾ cup stone-ground cornmeal, or blue cornmeal if you wish

1 to 2 teaspoons ground dried mild New Mexican red chile

1 teaspoon dried thyme

1 teaspoon salt, or more to taste

freshly milled black pepper

lemon wedges

1. Fry the bacon in a large heavy skillet over medium heat until brown and crisp. Drain the bacon, reserving it and the drippings in the skillet. Add oil as necessary to the drippings to measure a generous ¼ inch in the skillet.

2. Cut 2 moderately deep diagonal slashes into the sides of each fish. On a large plate stir together the cornmeal, chile, thyme, salt, and pepper. Roll each fish in the cornmeal mixture, pressing it into the slashes.

3. Warm the bacon drippings mixture over medium heat. Fry the fish, in batches if necessary, for 8 to 10 minutes or until the cornmeal is lightly browned and crunchy and the fish is flaky throughout, turning once. Serve the trout with bacon bits scattered over it and garnish with lemon wedges.

Mountain Trout Fillets, Fred Harvey Style

Restaurateur and hospitality icon Fred Harvey revolutionized dining on the western frontier in partnership with the Atchison, Topeka and Santa Fe Railway Company. One of their most astonishing joint projects was what today would be called a spa resort, the Montezuma, just outside of Las Vegas near the mouth of Gallinas Canyon. A six-mile spur railroad line took clients all the way to the door of the magnificent turreted Queen Anne–style hotel, now on the campus of the United World College. On opening night in 1886, this was one of the featured dishes. It followed turtle soup, made of turtles harvested in the Gulf of Mexico and kept alive at the Montezuma in an outdoor pool. The hotel, something of a monumental white elephant, went out of business by the time of statehood, but the trout preparation survived in other Fred Harvey kitchens. Though not an option from the streams of New Mexico, ruby trout fillets make a pretty contrast with the creamy horseradish sauce.

Serves 4

Poaching liquid

4 cups fish or seafood stock

⅔ cup minced shallots

8 black peppercorns

4 whole cloves

3 bay leaves

juice of 1 lemon plus lemon "shells"

¼ cup white vinegar

1 teaspoon salt

2 teaspoons unsalted butter

Horseradish cream

¾ cup whipping cream

½ teaspoon white vinegar

¼ teaspoon granulated sugar

pinch or 2 of salt

1½ to 3 teaspoons freshly grated horseradish, or more to taste

4 large or 8 small trout fillets

minced chives

For poaching liquid

1. Combine the ingredients in a medium saucepan. Bring the liquid to a boil, then reduce the heat to a simmer and cook for 15 minutes. Remove the pan from the heat, add the butter and let the liquid steep for about 15 minutes more.

For horseradish cream

1. While the poaching liquid cooks down, whisk together the cream, vinegar, sugar, and salt in a small bowl. Don't turn the mixture into whipped cream but whisk until it develops enough body to run off a spoon slowly. Stir in the horseradish. Refrigerate until time to serve.

Born in England, Fred Harvey started migrating west at the age of fifteen when he moved to New York. He worked in restaurants as a teenager, but the boom times in the railroad industry soon attracted the young entrepreneur and kept him heading toward new horizons as tracks gradually spread across the country toward the Pacific.

After settling in Leavenworth, Kansas, Harvey met the head of the Atchison, Topeka and Santa Fe Railway Company. The two men agreed in a handshake deal that Harvey would build and operate restaurants along the railroad route. The first lunch counters opened in 1876 and eventually grew by the time of Harvey's death into a hospitality empire comprising forty-seven restaurants, fifteen hotels, and thirty railroad dining cars.

A marketing genius, Harvey had a hand in the creation of hotel and restaurant chains, the early employment of women in a hosting capacity as the Harvey Girls, the development of the western souvenir trade, and one of the first efforts to sell Indian tourism to Americans. Some of his initiatives created heated controversy, but in New Mexico alone his company had businesses in Albuquerque, Belen, Carlsbad, Deming, Gallup, Lamy, Las Vegas, Raton, Rincon, Santa Fe, San Marcial, and Vaughn.

Assembly

1. You'll need a fish poacher, large skillet, or other pan that can hold the fillets in a single layer. A baking dish that can be placed over direct heat will work, too. (You can also poach the trout in a couple of batches, simply reusing the liquid.) Arrange fillets skin-side up in the poacher.

2. Pour the warm poaching liquid over the trout. If there's not enough liquid to cover the trout, add additional fish stock or water. Bring the mixture to a simmer over medium heat, then reduce the heat until the liquid has only occasional breaking bubbles around the edge and cover. Poach the trout for 5 minutes. Remove the poacher from the heat, uncover, and let fillets sit in the liquid for about 10 minutes, until cooked through and flaky.

3. Remove the trout carefully from the liquid with a wide fish spatula or other sturdy spatula. Arrange 1 or 2 fillets, skin-side down, on each plate. Serve right away with a spoonful of the horseradish cream and a sprinkling of chives.

Variations: This can be made with whole head-on trout; just double the amount of poaching liquid and increase the poaching time by several minutes. If you don't have fresh horseradish for the cream, you can use horseradish in a jar (but avoid varieties in beet juice). In this case, leave out the vinegar since canned versions of the pungent ingredient contain vinegar already.

7 Vegetables, Beans, and Side Dishes

Side dishes are among the most beloved favorites in New Mexican cooking, to such an extent that some of them are likely to appear on anyone's plate almost daily and at any time of the day. Pinto beans certainly fit in that class, and so does posole or rice depending on the area of the state, and during the harvest season in particular squash, corn, and green chile also show up regularly in various forms.

Some of the vegetable sides can be turned into vegetarian main-course dishes, but in their most common versions they are often cooked with a little meat or stock. Many New Mexicans historically ate vegetarian meals much of the time—just beans and tortillas in plenty of cases—but it was usually from necessity rather than choice in the past.

Our selection of sides focuses on everyday options, ignoring many other tasty choices that appear less frequently or come to the state from elsewhere. We love the broccoli and grape salad often found on Pueblo feast-day tables, the shishito peppers that now appear at our farmers' markets, fried green tomatoes, twice-baked potatoes, and scores of other sides, but we've limited ourselves here for the most part to time-honored New Mexican favorites.

Quelites

In Spanish *quelites* refers to tender greens, often wild varieties, but in New Mexico it's become the name for a type of foraged spinach known in English as lamb's-quarters. It's easy to spot the spiky-shaped leaf on gangly stems among the weeds in your yard or garden, but until you're sure what to look for, ask about it at a farmers' market or substitute regular spinach. As a dish, the greens are often rounded out with a large handful of universally popular pinto beans to add heft. During Lent, this combination often becomes a meatless main dish, sometimes with sliced hard-boiled egg placed on top. Our friend Fred Cisneros, graphic designer and co-owner of Santa Fe's Flying Tortilla Restaurant, reminisced for us about quelites. Both of his parents' families grew gardens with lots of spinach in the Costilla and Questa areas of northern New Mexico. Fred's mother, Elsie Martinez Cisneros, and his paternal grandmother, Eulogia Gonzales Cisneros, canned the spinach and used it throughout the year for their versions of quelites. Fred remembers that his sisters didn't care for it at all and his father, Fred Senior, would eat it occasionally, leaving most of it—happily—for Fred and his mom. His memories of the dish and its bacony aroma led him to add it to the menu at the Flying Tortilla.

Serves 4 to 6

2 tablespoons olive oil or bacon drippings

⅓ cup minced white onion

1 teaspoon crushed dried New Mexican red chile, with some seeds included

1½ pounds fresh lamb's-quarters leaves or spinach leaves, still damp from cleaning, or 12 ounces thawed frozen spinach

1 to 1½ cups drained cooked whole pinto beans, such as Frijoles de Olla (page 126)

salt

vinegar, optional

Wild Things

The Pueblo and Diné settlers in the Southwest enjoyed a different kind of wild spinach that grows uncultivated in New Mexico, the Rocky Mountain bee plant. They boiled its iron-rich leaves and stems to make hard cakes that stored well for winter consumption. It's recognizable in summer from its pink, purple, and white flowers.

Another summer green free for the taking, verdolagas (or purslane), can be sautéed like quelites with a little onion or garlic. You eat both the fleshy leaves and stems, which hug the ground, competing in our own largely untended back lot with tufts of native grass. Expect an almost lemony tang.

Wild celery (or chimaja) and wild asparagus are other New Mexico favorites, used in similar fashion to their domestic counterparts. All of these wild plants are most common around sources of water, often springing up along acequias or in fields they irrigate. Be sure to avoid them from anywhere near a road, where they may have been subject to car exhaust, and never eat anything that you can't positively identify.

1. Warm the oil over medium heat in a high-sided skillet or Dutch oven. Stir in the onion and sauté several minutes, until translucent. Stir in the chile and cook for 30 seconds. Add the lamb's-quarters. Cover, reduce the heat to medium low, and cook for about 5 minutes, until the greens are well wilted but still deep green.

2. Stir in pinto beans and heat through. Add salt. If necessary, cook the mixture for another 1 or 2 minutes uncovered to reduce any accumulated liquid.

3. Transfer the quelites to a serving dish. Serve hot, accompanied if you wish by vinegar.

Variations: Garbanzo beans, once common in New Mexican cooking, can substitute for the pintos. If you want to take the dish back to its most elemental form, you can also leave out the beans entirely. If you like the idea of adding a little meat, start by frying up about four ounces of chorizo, which may eliminate the need for any oil at all.

Calabacitas

In high summer in New Mexico, people eat this sauté by the bowlful. It is essentially *the* fresh vegetable preparation universal to cooks throughout the state. The diminuitive name "calabacitas" refers to the summer squash, always a key ingredient in the dish, usually with corn and green chile for extra flavor and texture. Some cooks would dry sliced "little wheels," or *rueditas*, of the squash for the winter, and you can still find these sold in bags at the end of the growing season in some farmers' markets. The preparation for calabacitas is fast, easy, and forgiving of additions and subtractions of ingredients. Just don't rush the cooking because the squash should be quite tender when done.

Serves 6

2 tablespoons butter

2 tablespoons vegetable oil

2 pounds mixed summer squash (such as small zucchini, yellow crooked-neck or gold bar squash, and light-green-skinned calabacita), sliced thin or in bite-size cubes

1 medium onion, chopped

2 small tomatoes, preferably Roma or Italian plum, optional

2 cups corn kernels, fresh or frozen

¼ to ¾ cup chopped, roasted mild New Mexican green chile, fresh or thawed frozen

½ teaspoon salt

up to ¼ cup half-and-half, optional

4 ounces (1 cup) shredded Monterey Jack or cheddar cheese, optional

1. Warm the butter and oil in a large skillet over medium heat. Add the squash, onion, and optional tomatoes. Sauté for 10 to 15 minutes, until the squash is well softened. Stir in the corn, chiles, and salt, and cook covered for another 10 minutes until all vegetables are tender. Pour in the half-and-half if you wish and simmer briefly, until the liquid is reduced by about half.

2. Serve hot. If using the cheese, scatter it over the calabacitas just before serving.

Variations: Expect about as many versions as there are cooks in the state. One of the first uses we've seen in a New Mexico cookbook for fresh cilantro was in Calavacitas con Chile Verde in Philomena Romero's *New Mexican Dishes* (1970). She suggests the option of "1 sprig fresh corriander." In a version from the Los Alamos Historical Society cookbook *Savoring the Past* (2001), San Ildefonso cook and potter Dora Tse-Pe sautéed pork sausage with the squash and then baked the mixture all together briefly before serving. The owners of Dick's Café in Las Cruces, the Perez family, make a very saucy version of calabacitas, rich with tomatoes, tomato sauce, and a heavier topping of cheese. Antoinette Gonzales Knight, whose parents founded Mary & Tito's in Albuquerque in the 1960s, says her dad liked to add ground sirloin. We've seen embellishments of carrots and chicos, substitutions of goat cheese for the cheddar or Monterey Jack, olive oil as the cooking fat, and flavoring additions such as garlic, cinnamon, and fresh mint.

Squash Blossoms

Where squash grows, so do golden squash blossoms, one of summer's fleeting delicacies. They are so coveted in New Mexico that some farmers choose the variety of squash they plant by the desirability of its blossoms for stuffing. The flowers wither away quickly to nothing, so they are typically harvested on the day of cooking. If picking your own, choose just the male blossoms (the ones with the distinctive male protrusion at their heart), leaving the females to bear squash. You can add them, simply sliced into ribbons, to sautés such as the preceding calabacitas or to scrambled eggs or omelets. Most often they are fried, sometimes with a cheese filling as we do here.

Serves 4 to 6

Filling

4 ounces fresh goat cheese, softened

4 ounces shredded Monterey Jack cheese

½ teaspoon crumbled dried Mexican oregano or marjoram

12 large very fresh squash blossoms (with several inches of stem attached, if possible) swished in water and allowed to dry on paper towels

Batter

1 cup all-purpose flour

1 tablespoon dried ground mild New Mexican red chile

1 teaspoon baking powder

1 teaspoon salt

¾ teaspoon ground coriander, optional

¾ teaspoon ground cinnamon, optional

1 large egg, lightly beaten

1 cup beer or club soda

vegetable oil for deep-frying

For the filling and blossoms

1. Combine the goat cheese, Monterey Jack, and oregano (or marjoram) in a small bowl.

2. Pinch out and discard the stamen from inside each blossom. Gently stuff each blossom with a portion of the filling and wrap the blossom snugly around the filling, pressing it against the moist cheese.

<hr>

Zucchini Market

Once upon a time the Santa Fe Farmers' Market was what I call a Zucchini Market. A Zucchini Market is what takes place after your refrigerator is full of zucchini, and after your friends and neighbors begin refusing generous gifts of zucchini, and after the chickens begin pecking at other things. This is when the collective intelligence declares that it's time to start opening up the Farmers' Market.

Recent arrivals to Santa Fe are astounded when I tell them that back in the 1970s the Farmers' Market didn't open until the last week in July, which is when zucchini, corn, and beans begin producing in abundance.

Mind you, that was before salad was introduced to Northern New Mexico . . .

—STANLEY CRAWFORD, *THE RIVER IN WINTER: NEW AND SELECTED ESSAYS* (2003)

For the batter

1. Stir together the dry ingredients in a medium bowl. Mix in the egg and beer (or club soda).

Assembly

1. Fill a heavy pan with at least 2 inches of oil. Heat the oil to 350° F. Set a baking rack over paper towels near the stovetop.

2. Dip the blossoms into the batter, coating them lightly but thoroughly. Let excess batter drain back into bowl. If the blossoms have stems, use them as a handle of sorts. Lay the blossoms gently into the oil a few at a time. Fry them for about 1 minute, until crisp and golden, turning as needed. Drain and serve as soon as all the blossoms are fried, 2 or 3 to a portion.

Green Chile Tempura

Shohko and Hiro Fukuda arrived in the United States from Japan during the era of the "flower children." Like many others of their generation, they roamed the country for months by Volkswagen minibus. When they arrived in northern New Mexico, they knew they had found their future home. Before leaving Japan, Shohko and Hiro had studied with George Ohsawa, founder of the macrobiotic diet and philosophy. Their knowledge of the subject led them to open a natural foods store in Santa Fe and eventually to found Shohko Café, still going strong today with the help of their daughters. The couple's fascination with chiles rellenos inspired them to create green chile tempura, now also found on many other menus around the state.

Serves 4 or more

Dipping sauce

¼ cup plus 2 tablespoons
    soy sauce

3 tablespoons mirin (Japanese
    sweetened rice wine)

1½ teaspoons rice vinegar

1 teaspoon grated daikon radish,
    fresh ginger, or both, optional

Tempura

6 fresh whole mild to medium
    New Mexican green chiles

vegetable oil for deep-frying

1 tablespoon toasted sesame oil

1 large egg yolk

1½ cups ice water

1½ cups cake flour (divided use)

For the sauce

1. Stir together the soy sauce, mirin, and rice vinegar in a small bowl. If you wish, stir in daikon or ginger or both.

For the tempura

1. Roast the chiles over a stove burner, turning them with tongs as needed to blacken and blister them on all sides. Place the chiles into a plastic bag to steam until cool enough to handle. Peel the chiles, wearing rubber gloves if your skin is sensitive. Strip away the blackened peel, using paper towels to get off as much as possible. Rinse your fingers as necessary. Slice each chile in half vertically and discard the stem and seeds. Cut each chile half crosswise into 2 pieces.

2. Pour about 3 inches of vegetable oil into a deep skillet, then add the sesame oil. Heat the oil to 375° F. Place a baking rack over several thicknesses of paper towels near the stovetop.

When Shohko and Hiro developed green chile tempura, they applied the techniques of their own Japanese cuisine to the iconic ingredient of New Mexico. At the same time they continued to focus in their home and café on more traditional dishes from their mother country, a pattern that has prevailed among most immigrants from the days of the first French fur traders who settled around Mora and Las Vegas in the early nineteenth century.

Asians came to New Mexico to labor on the railroad and in agriculture, and our famous French archbishop, Jean-Baptiste Lamy, brought in Italian stonemasons to work on our churches. Jews established thriving mercantile businesses in the capital, while Greek miners migrated to the mountains. As far back as the Gadsden Purchase in 1853, Mexicans on the northern side of the line suddenly found themselves to be New Mexicans, and in recent decades in particular more of their countrymen have followed them into the United States. Many of these immigrants have introduced their home cuisines in restaurants across the state, especially in Albuquerque, an increasingly cosmopolitan city for dining.

3. While the oil heats, mix the batter. First whisk together the egg yolk and ice water until quite frothy. Whisk in 1¼ cups of cake flour, just until lightly blended. Don't overwork the batter. A few streaks or lumps of flour are fine. The batter will be thin.

4. Dump the remaining ¼ cup flour into a shallow bowl.

5. When the oil reaches 375° F, immediately dunk the chile pieces, a few at a time, into the dish of flour, then dip in the batter and slip into the oil. Cook for 3 to 4 minutes, turning as needed, until just golden. Drain on the baking rack. Repeat with the remaining chile pieces and batter, adding as many to the oil as you can without crowding and dropping the oil temperature. Serve immediately with the sauce.

Baked Pumpkin

Part of the corn, bean, and squash trinity that underpins New Mexican cooking, pumpkins play a much larger role in the state historically than as a Thanksgiving pie filling. In the fall they were sliced, like other squash, into strips and dried for winter meals. Eaten fresh, they are often baked with sugar and spice, as in this Chimayó version that dates back at least six decades. Tiny, individual-serving-size pumpkins such as Little Jack Horners are particularly enchanting for the dish. Other winter squash, such as acorn varieties, are equally tasty and slice easily into equal wedges for baking.

Serves 6

3-pound pumpkin, seeded
   and sliced in 6 wedges, or
   6 miniature single-serving
   pumpkins, tops cut off jack-
   o'-lantern style and seeded

vegetable oil

salt to taste

6 tablespoons butter

¼ cup packed brown sugar

½ teaspoon ground canela or
   other cinnamon

¼ teaspoon ground dried New
   Mexican red chile

¼ teaspoon ground dried
   coriander

1. Preheat the oven to 350° F.

2. Place the pumpkin wedges or baby pumpkins (with lids on) in a shallow baking dish. Coat thinly with oil, sprinkle with salt, and bake for 50 to 55 minutes, until soft.

3. In a small pan, melt the butter and mix it with the remaining ingredients. Keep the mixture warm.

4. Spoon the butter mixture over the pumpkin wedges or drizzle inside the baby pumpkins, replacing their lids afterward. Bake for an additional 10 to 15 minutes until the pumpkin is soft. Serve hot.

Papas con Chile

When a chill edges into late-summer nights, signaling that autumn is going to overtake us, this zesty combination of potatoes cooked down with green chile and tomatoes makes the perfect segue. While any grocery-store russet works for this, we like the heritage canela russet potato variety originally grown in Colorado's high San Luis Valley. Years ago, New Mexican farmers traded their chile for beans and seed potatoes from the San Luis, just over New Mexico's northern border, and they now raise the russets themselves.

Serves 6 or more

4 russet potatoes, about 12 ounces each, peeled and cut into 2-inch chunks

1 tablespoon salt, or more to taste

water

1 cup chopped, roasted mild New Mexican green chile, fresh or thawed frozen

3 small to medium tomatoes, preferably Roma or Italian plum, diced

2 garlic cloves, minced

2 cups chicken stock

1. Place the potatoes and 1 tablespoon of salt in a saucepan and cover with water by at least 1 inch. Cook the potatoes over moderate heat until they are just barely tender, about 15 minutes, and drain them.

2. Return the pan with potatoes to moderate heat for 1 minute to let some of the moisture evaporate. Stir in the remaining ingredients. Cook the potatoes over medium heat for about 15 to 20 minutes, stirring up from the bottom frequently, until the potatoes become soft and a thick sauce has formed.

3. Taste and add more salt as needed. Serve warm.

Frijoles de Olla

A pot (or olla) of beans burbling lazily on the back of the stove is one of the bedrock foundations of New Mexican cooking. Gardeners and farmers grow dozens of varieties of beans today, including oval bolitas, speckled Anasazis, and favas (or habas), but it's the earthy pinto that reigns supreme. Any of these beans can be simmered simply in salted water with tasty results. For pintos, though, we suggest using the seasoning combination favored by Noe Cano, the longtime kitchen manager at the Santa Fe School of Cooking, who makes the best frijoles we've ever eaten.

Serves 6 to 8

2 cups dried pinto beans

8 cups water, or more as needed

1 head of garlic, minced

2 dried chipotle chiles

2 teaspoons dried epazote or
   1 tablespoon minced fresh
   epazote, optional

1½ teaspoons salt, or more
   to taste

1. Pick through the beans and rinse them, discarding any gravel or grit.

2. Place the beans in a stockpot or large heavy saucepan. Cover them with water and add the garlic, chipotles, and optional epazote.

3. Bring the beans just to a boil over high heat, then reduce the heat to low and simmer the beans uncovered. Plan on a total cooking time of 2 to 2¼ hours. After 1 hour, stir the beans up from the bottom and check the water level. If there is not at least an inch more water than beans, add enough hot water to bring it up to that level. Check the beans after another 30 minutes, repeating the process. Add the salt after the beans are well softened and continue simmering. Check every 15 minutes, keeping the level of the water just above the beans. There should be extra liquid at the completion of the cooking time, but the beans should not be watery. If you wish, remove ½ to 1 cup of the beans, mash them, and return them to the pot for a thicker liquid.

4. Serve warm. The beans keep several days and are even better reheated.

TIP

How to Cook Beans

When cooking beans, keep in mind the old expression "*No hay como la lumbre mansa.*" ("There is nothing like a slow fire.") You want the beans to become soft and creamy while holding their shape, and any attempt to speed the cooking tends to disintegrate them instead. The time required depends on the altitude—the higher, the longer—plus the general obstinacy and age of the beans (look for ones labeled "new crop"). Many cooks soak the beans before cooking, but we've realized that the step steals some of the flavor and doesn't significantly reduce the time on the stove. A pressure cooker is the only thing that speeds up the process. For conventional cooking, use a heavy pan. If you intend to cook beans frequently, consider buying a local clay pot. Bean pots (ollas) made from New Mexico's micaceous clay, which add their own earthy character to the flavor, are treasures to be handed down from one generation to another. Pots made by Felipe Ortega in the traditional coiled and scraped Jicarilla Apache style are particularly sought after. They can be acquired through Café Pasqual's Gallery in Santa Fe (www. pasquals.com).

On Labor Day weekend in 2010 the small town of Wagon Mound in the northeast corner of the state celebrated the centennial edition of its annual Bean Days festival. It all started one century earlier when Higinio Gonzales and his crew cooked up a big batch of pinto beans in washtubs behind the schoolhouse and invited everyone in the vicinity to the feast.

In those days pinto beans were a major crop of the area, and even though that has changed the community maintains the old tradition in an updated format. The washtubs are gone, replaced now with a large pit dug in the ground. A wood-and-charcoal fire blazes in the pit on the first afternoon to heat the underground oven, beans and beef for barbecuing go in around dusk, metal panels cover the food, and earth is piled on top. The next day the beans and beef are dug out and served to about fifteen hundred guests. The weekend continues with a street dance, a parade, a couple of special masses, horseshoe and baseball tournaments, and a rodeo.

Variations: In southern New Mexico, cooks often turn their pintos into refried beans. To accomplish this, melt a couple of tablespoons of bacon fat or lard—okay, even vegetable oil—in a skillet. Sauté a chopped small onion and a couple of minced garlic cloves until soft and then add a couple of cups of whole beans with some of their cooking liquid. Smash the beans with a potato masher or Mexican-style bean masher roughly, leaving some texture, and cook until the beans become a thick paste. Some say the test of readiness and quality in refries is being thick enough for a fork to stand up in them. Serve hot, topped with shredded cheese if you wish.

Posole

As one of the trinity of special summer crops, corn is occasionally eaten in New Mexico in ways familiar to other Americans, such as roasted or grilled on the cob, or made into a summer pudding, or simply cooked as a side dish of buttered kernels. The characteristically local ways of preparing corn, however, start with converting it to a preserved form. Turning it into posole is the most common method. The corn is treated with slaked lime, or nixtamalized, to remove its outer skin, a technique developed by Native Americans centuries ago. The corn puffs up and becomes somewhat slicker in texture, with a distinctive toothsomeness when cooked. The technique also makes the vitamins and an essential amino acid in the plant accessible when eating the corn. A similar process produces hominy, but the lime compound is somewhat different and doesn't result in the same earthiness found in posole. In some ways posole comes close to being a sacred dish in New Mexico. It's almost always served on Saint's Day feasts at the Pueblos and at Christmas and New Year's gatherings of families and friends.

Serves 8 or more

6 dried New Mexican red chile pods, stemmed and seeded

1 to 1½ pounds pork shoulder or loin, trimmed of surface fat and cut in bite-size cubes, or 1 or 2 pigs' feet

water

2 pounds frozen posole or 1 pound dried posole

2 medium onions, chopped

6 to 10 garlic cloves, minced

1 tablespoon plus 1 teaspoon salt, or more to taste

1. If you will be using frozen posole, first combine the chile pods with the pork in a Dutch oven or large pot and simmer in 4 quarts of water for about 30 minutes. Then add the frozen posole and cook about 30 minutes more. If your posole is dried, add it with the chile, pork, and 6 quarts of water and simmer for about 1 hour.

2. Stir in the onions, garlic, and salt and continue to simmer over a low fire until the posole is soft. Expect the remaining cooking to take another 30 minutes for frozen posole and at least 1 hour if dried. Do not be surprised if it takes a bit longer.

3. Serve hot in bowls with some of the liquid, or drain it with a slotted spoon and serve it on the side with other plated foods.

A Posole Fantasy

I want you to know that when I had the idea of opening a Northern New Mexican restaurant in Manhattan, I was way ahead of the curve. This was, after all, in 1971. I had returned to New York after a summer in New Mexico . . . inspired to hatch a scheme for creating a steady source of quality posole in Manhattan. . . . In Northern New Mexican homes, posole is traditionally served during the Christmas season. My restaurant scheme was based on the desire to eat it every day of the year."

—CALVIN TRILLIN, "BOWLFUL OF DREAMS," *GOURMET* (OCTOBER 2002)

Variations: New Mexicans eat posole for both everyday and celebratory occasions. Everyday versions, like this, served on the side perhaps with enchiladas, may have been cooked with a little pork or other meat, but posole for Pueblo feast days or Christmas Eve parties often includes hefty amounts of pork feet, heads, or ribs, or maybe beef neck bones or oxtails. In Mexico, where the dish is spelled "pozole," it's normally a complete special-occasion meal on its own and comes with a dozen or so small plates of garnishes and seasonings to add to your already heaping bowl. In southern New Mexico you sometimes find this kind of embellishment in a more limited way, even with the everyday posole offered at the famous La Posta de Mesilla restaurant. If you want to make this a more summery dish, leave out the red chile pods, and in the last 30 minutes of cooking, toss in some fresh corn kernels, bits of carrot or scallion tops, and ½ to 1 cup chopped roasted mild to medium New Mexican green chile. If you wish, garnish with chopped cilantro.

Chicos

Usually made with young "green" field corn, chicos are typically slow-roasted in outdoor horno ovens and then dried on rooftops. Farmers start a wood fire in the horno, and when the oven walls reach the right temperature, they rake out the embers with a hoe, place moistened corn in its husks inside, seal the door and vent hole, and leave the corn to roast overnight. The ears emerge the next morning with a prized light smokiness. In many areas chicos have become a nearly lost classic, only available at some farmers' markets, old-fashioned general stores, and specialty shops like the Santa Fe School of Cooking, but they are definitely worth a major search effort. When dried, they keep well for months, and when cooked the chicos burst with smoky, slightly chewy goodness, offering a quite different taste and texture than posole.

Serves 8

2 tablespoons vegetable oil	2 bay leaves, optional
2 medium onions, minced	6 cups chicken stock
4 garlic cloves, minced	½ cup chopped roasted mild
1¾ to 2 cups chicos	green New Mexican chile,
1 teaspoon salt, or more to taste	fresh or thawed frozen

1. In a large saucepan or Dutch oven, warm the oil over medium heat. Stir in the onions and garlic and sauté until soft, 8 to 10 minutes.

2. Add the chicos, salt, optional bay leaves, and stock, and bring to a boil. Reduce the heat to a simmer and cook uncovered for 1½ to 2 hours, or until the chicos are well softened and have lost their raw, starchy flavor. They will remain a little chewy and crunchy. Add water if the chicos begin to dry out. Add the chile and a little more salt if needed and cook for another 15 to 20 minutes. The chicos should have some liquid but should not be extremely soupy.

3. Serve hot in small bowls with some of the liquid or drain with a slotted spoon and serve plated beside other dishes.

Variations: We tend to like the subtle corn flavor without meat, but beef short ribs or cubed lamb stew meat are not uncommon additions. Cooked chicos can be mixed half and half with pinto beans or other varieties of beans, or added to soups or stews.

"Old, but Good, New Mexico Ways"

Fabian Garcia, the first researcher in New Mexico State University's Chile Pepper Breeding and Genetics Program, also promoted chico production in a July 1917 article in *The New Mexico Farm Courier*. He encouraged farmers across the state to build horno ovens and take up the "old, but good, New Mexico ways of drying roasting ears."

He said, "Take the roasting ears and place them in the oven or right in the fire, without removing the husks, and let them cook until done. Then remove the husk and allow the roasting ear to dry. . . . In preparing large numbers of roasting ears by this method, a good way is to build a large adobe oven and heat it thoroughly; remove the coals, throw in the roasting ears with the husks on, immediately close the oven tightly, and let the corn remain in it all night. The next morning the corn can be taken out and, after removing the husks, placed out to dry, shelled or on the cob."

Blue Corn Marbles

If you think chicos or fideos are unusual side dishes, you've probably never tried blue corn marbles. In her fascinating Zuni Pueblo cookbook *Idonapshe: Let's Eat: Traditional Zuni Foods* (1999), Rita Edaakie tells how to make a special traditional blue food coloring from limestone rocks to use in dishes such as piki bread, blue cornmeal patties, and blue corn marbles.

She combines the coloring with cornmeal, rolls the dough into marble-size rounds, and boils the balls, suggesting they be served as a side dish with steak or green tomatoes. Just don't eat them in the summer. Zuni lore suggests they may bring on hailstorms at that time of the year.

Sopa de Fideos

This *sopa* isn't what most people would call a soup. Technically, it's a *sopa seca*, or dry soup, a dish cooked in a healthy quantity of liquid that gets mostly absorbed. You can make your own vermicelli-like fideos, as Cleofas M. Jaramillo discusses in her cookbook *The Genuine New Mexico Tasty Recipes* (1939), where she rolls out pasta dough "into long shoestrings," but most cooks today buy fideos beside spaghetti and other noodles at supermarkets. Sometimes it comes broken into pieces and other times is sold in coiled nests of longer strands. Kids love fideos.

Serves 4 as a main dish, 6 as a side dish

2 tablespoons olive oil or bacon drippings

1 small onion, minced

10 ounces fideos or vermicelli, broken into pieces 1 to 2 inches in length if not sold that way

1 garlic clove, minced

2½ cups beef or chicken stock or water

1 medium tomato, chopped fine, optional

¼ cup piñon nuts, toasted, optional

chopped fresh mint, optional

1. Warm the oil in a heavy skillet over medium heat. Add the onion and sauté about 3 minutes until translucent. Stir in the crumbled fideos and garlic and continue cooking several more minutes until the pasta is mostly golden brown.

2. Add the stock or water and optional tomato. Cover the pan, reduce the heat to a low simmer, and cook until the liquid is nearly absorbed and the fideos are tender, about 15 minutes. Let sit covered for an additional couple of minutes.

3. Garnish with piñon nuts or mint, if you like, and serve.

Spanish Rice

Historically, side dishes of corn and beans are much more common than rice in New Mexico, partially at least because the state is too arid for rice cultivation. This has become a contemporary favorite in southern New Mexico, though, and is now so common on combination plates in other parts of the Southwest that some northern restaurants offer it as well. There's nothing Spanish about it, of course, and not much Mexican either, but it's a stellar example of a dish that good home cooks can prepare much better than any production kitchen.

Serves 4

1 tablespoon bacon drippings or vegetable oil

¼ cup minced onion

2 garlic cloves, minced

1 cup uncooked rice

1 cup water

14½- to 15-ounce can diced tomatoes (preferably a fire-roasted variety), with juice

1 teaspoon salt

½ to 1 teaspoon ground dried mild New Mexican red chile

1. Warm the bacon drippings in a large saucepan over medium heat. Add the onion and sauté until soft, about 5 minutes. Mix in the garlic and rice and cook several minutes until the rice turns translucent.

2. Pour the water and tomatoes into the rice. Sprinkle in salt and chile, and stir once to incorporate. Reduce the heat, cover the pan, and simmer the mixture for 15 to 18 minutes, until all the liquid is absorbed. Remove the pan from the heat and let the rice steam covered for 5 to 10 minutes.

3. Fluff rice with a fork and serve warm.

Variations: We like to make this a heartier dish with the addition of ground lamb. Skip the bacon drippings and sauté the meat, adding the onion and garlic to it after it has lost its raw color, and continue as the recipe recommends.

Rice with Yerba Buena and Azafrán

In the past New Mexico cooks typically flavored imported rice with local seasonings such as mint and safflower, the latter a New Mexico substitute for once scarce and always pricey saffron. Personally, we prefer this lightly scented dish over Spanish rice on most occasions. At the risk of being old-fashioned but satisfied, give it a try.

Serves 4

2 cups chicken stock

⅓ cup loosely packed mint leaves

1 tablespoon bacon drippings or vegetable oil

2 tablespoons minced onion

2 garlic cloves, minced

1 cup uncooked rice

1 teaspoon salt

1 teaspoon New Mexican azafrán (safflower stamens) or a pinch of saffron

¾ teaspoon ground dried mild New Mexican red chile

1 tablespoon minced fresh mint

1. Bring the stock and mint leaves to a boil in a small saucepan. Remove the pan from the heat and let steep 10 to 15 minutes.

2. Warm the bacon drippings in a large saucepan over medium heat. Add the onion and garlic and sauté until soft. Mix in the rice and cook until translucent.

3. Strain the stock (discarding mint leaves) and pour it into the rice. Sprinkle in salt, azafrán or saffron, and chile and stir once to incorporate. Reduce the heat, cover the pan, and simmer for 15 to 18 minutes, until all the liquid is absorbed. Remove the pan from the heat, sprinkle in the minced mint, cover the pan, and let sit for 5 to 10 minutes.

4. Fluff the rice with a fork and serve warm.

8 Breads and Tortillas

Bread and its components have always been more important in New Mexico than in most of the United States. It's not because of its role as a basic food, long appreciated everywhere in the country, but rather the spiritual power that New Mexicans attribute to cornmeal and wheat and the simple breads made of those elements.

Pueblo farmers have cultivated corn for many centuries, of course, long before the arrival of the Spanish. In Pueblo religious ceremonies, cornmeal is set out in the morning to ask the sun to bless the day and it also becomes a part of prayers for rain in the summer and snow in the winter. Even the grinding of corn to make the meal may take on sacred significance with the chanting of ritual songs.

Holy Communion for Spanish Catholic settlers gave bread made of wheat flour a similar reverential role, with the priest offering it symbolically as the body of Christ. For the devoted Spanish parishioners of New Mexico, taking the Eucharist represented a genuine reenactment of the Lord's Supper, Christ's last meal before his arrest and crucifixion. The colonists planted wheat as soon as they unpacked their wagons, and their heirs continued to raise it on family plots in the northern part of the state until recent times.

In most modern meals, bread seems almost like an afterthought. You can get that impression in New Mexico as well as elsewhere but never so fully. The old associations still survive in the communal memory and continue to endow our breads with a special sense of place and timelessness.

Blue Corn Tortillas

The Puebloans made a variety of simple corn breads before the arrival of the Spanish, probably including blue corn tortillas similar to these. Despite ancient roots, blue cornmeal remained virtually unknown outside of northern New Mexico until the 1980s, when chef-promoted forms of Southwest cuisine became a national fad. Pueblo leaders chafed at what they considered spiritual disrespect for their heritage, but feelings tempered over time as other Americans acknowledged the beautifully earthy taste and praised the Pueblo farmers for their ingenuity. Blue cornmeal makes a fragile dough on its own, so it's common to bolster it with white or yellow masa harina. Look for "tortilla-grind" masa harina or the finest grind that a market sells. Most cooks use an inexpensive tortilla press for flattening the dough, but you might want to try patting out a few by hand just to see what skill it really requires.

Makes 1 dozen 5- to 6-inch tortillas

1 cup fine-ground blue cornmeal or blue masa harina	½ teaspoon salt
1 cup fine-ground (white or yellow) masa harina	1¼ cups warm water, or more as needed

1. Mix the ingredients in a shallow bowl with your hands until the dough is smooth. The dough should be quite moist but hold its shape. Add a little more water or masa harina if needed to achieve the proper consistency.

2. Form the dough into 12 balls approximately 1½ inches in diameter. Cover the balls with plastic wrap if not making the tortillas immediately.

3. Heat a dry griddle or heavy skillet over medium-high heat.

4. Line a basket (preferably a lidded tortilla basket) with a cloth napkin.

5. Place 1 ball of dough in a tortilla press between the 2 sheets of plastic sometimes sold with the press or use a pair of pint or quart plastic sandwich bags. Press the ball until it is flattened to the desired thickness, generally about ⅛ inch. Carefully pull the plastic from the round of dough and lay the dough on the hot griddle or skillet. Cook the tortilla for 30 seconds. Flip it and cook it for 1 minute on its second side. Then flip it back over to cook about 30 seconds longer on the first side. The tortilla will be speckled with brown flecks.

The Last of the Neighborhood Groceries

Johnnie's Cash Store may not be the very last family-owned neighborhood market in the whole of New Mexico, but it's the sole survivor today of the eighty or so similar groceries that used to exist in Santa Fe. Johnnie Armijo, now in his eighties, still mans the counter every day except Sunday. His father, Orlando, opened the store in 1946, and the two of them built it together at 420 Camino Don Miguel one adobe brick at a time.

Originally, like many neighborhood ventures, the shop carried clothes, radios, and other merchandise along with fresh meat and canned goods. Now the focus is strictly food, including take-out items such as the famous tamales, praised by even the restaurant critic of The Washington Post. Johnnie gets the tamales from a home cook in La Puebla who chooses to remain anonymous. Stop by for one the next time you're in the 'hood.

6. Cover the cooked tortillas to keep them warm while the remaining balls of dough are shaped and cooked. Serve warm in the basket with butter or salsa or reserve for another use. The tortillas taste best the day they are made.

Working ahead: The dough can be made into the individual balls up to several hours ahead as long as it is kept tightly covered. To reheat corn tortillas made earlier in the day, wrap a stack of them in a clean towel and put the package in a steamer. When steam begins to escape from the lid, turn off the heat and let the tortillas sit covered for 10 to 15 minutes. They'll keep warm this way for about 1 hour.

Variations: To make yellow or white corn tortillas, all you need is finely ground masa harina and water. Any corn tortilla dough is extremely forgiving since it has no wheat gluten to toughen it. To make 12 tortillas, combine 2 cups of masa harina, ½ teaspoon of salt, and about 1¼ cups of warm water. Form and cook them just as above. Many cooks go out of their way to find a special masa harina for corn tortillas. They seldom bother to grind the corn themselves anymore, but they often seek out a personal source for what they consider the most desirable texture and flavor. Some combine 2 or more masa harinas to create their own blend.

Flour Tortillas

In Southwest culinary circles, flour tortillas are most closely associated with the cooking of Arizona and the Mexican state of Sonora. New Mexican versions—thicker, smaller in diameter, and chewier than most others—actually probably predate these better-known cousins. Spanish settlers preferred wheat to corn, so they used it to produce a flatbread similar to a Pueblo tortilla, a tradition that has persisted in Hispano families for centuries now. Cheryl's Little Sister in the Big Brothers Big Sisters program, Lenore Tapia Baker, with other members of the Tapia family, taught us how to make these thirty years ago through a process of trial and many errors. Experienced practitioners can flap and slap and pull the dough out into perfect rounds, but for the rest of us it's usually easier to roll them out.

Makes about 8 tortillas, approximately 7 to 8 inches in diameter

2 cups low-gluten pastry or biscuit flour, or all-purpose flour

1½ teaspoons baking powder (reduce by ¼ teaspoon at altitudes above 5,000 feet)

1 teaspoon salt

1 tablespoon lard, vegetable shortening, or vegetable oil

¾ cup lukewarm water

unsalted butter or your favorite salsa

1. Sift together into a large bowl the flour, baking powder, and salt. Work in the lard with your fingers. Add the water, working it quickly until a sticky dough forms.

2. Knead the dough vigorously on a floured board for 1 minute. The mixture should no longer be sticky. This will sound a little odd, but if the dough is the same softness as your earlobe, it's ready. If it remains more firm, knead a few more strokes until it's earlobe soft. Cover the dough with a damp clean dish towel and let it rest for about 15 minutes.

TIP

How to Roll Flour Tortillas

• A rolling pin is okay for an occasional batch of tortillas, but it's really too heavy for the tender dough. To make them regularly, you'll want an inexpensive tortilla roller. The roller looks like, and in some households is, a short section of broomstick. Mexican markets usually carry them, and the Santa Fe School of Cooking (www.santafeschoolofcooking.com, 505-983-4511) sells them by mail order.

• Once you have flattened the balls of dough, roll them out from the center and turn the dough about a quarter-turn between rolls.

• To avoid toughening the dough, don't roll over the same spot more than a couple of times.

3. Divide the dough into 8 equal pieces and form into balls. Cover the balls again with the damp towel and let them rest for another 15 to 30 minutes. (The dough can be refrigerated at this stage and held for up to 4 hours. Bring the dough back to room temperature before proceeding.)

4. Roll out each dough ball, from the center, on a floured surface into a circle no thicker than ¼ inch. (The tortillas will puff up in thickness from the baking powder.) Turn the dough a quarter turn after each roll, to help shape the tortilla as you go. Trim off any ragged edges and discard them.

5. Line a basket or plate just larger than the tortillas with a cloth napkin or several thicknesses of paper napkins. Warm a dry griddle or large cast-iron skillet over high heat.

6. Cook the tortillas 30 seconds on each side, until the dough looks dry, slightly leathery, and speckled brown in a few spots. Place each tortilla immediately in the basket as it is cooked. Savor the tortillas warm, with butter or salsa, or reserve for another use.

Variations: The Junior League ladies of Albuquerque, who put together the ever-popular *Simply Simpatico* in 1981, included a tasty recipe they called Santa Fe Tortillas. Substitute bacon drippings for the lard and increase the amount to 3 tablespoons. Use buttermilk as the liquid in place of water. Cook over medium instead of high heat for about 2 minutes per side.

Horno-Style Bread

Pueblo cooks use outdoor adobe horno ovens more often than other New Mexicans today, but in the past almost everyone baked in them. Moors from the arid lands of North Africa introduced the beehive-shaped ovens to the Spanish, who brought the idea with them to New Mexico. Even after commercial yeast and gas stoves became available before statehood, most New Mexicans continued to bake in hornos, and they still enjoy the style of white wheat bread the earthen ovens produce.

Makes 1 1-pound loaf

1½ cups water

1 tablespoon lard or vegetable shortening, plus more for greasing the bowl

1 to 2 teaspoons sugar, optional

approximately 2½ cups sifted all-purpose flour

1 package rapid-rise dry yeast

1½ teaspoons salt

1 teaspoon crumbled dried sage, optional

1. Warm the water, fat, and optional sugar in a small saucepan over medium heat until the fat is melted. Pour the liquid into the bowl of a sturdy mixer with a dough hook and cool to lukewarm, about 110° F.

2. Add to the bowl 2 cups of the flour and the yeast, salt, and optional sage. Beat several minutes, adding as much of the remaining flour as necessary to make a smooth elastic dough with a satiny sheen. (Alternatively, combine the flour mixture as in step 1 in a large mixing bowl, add the liquid ingredients, and work with your fingers until the dough forms a cohesive, somewhat sticky ball. Turn the dough out onto a floured surface. Knead it several minutes, adding as much of the remaining flour as necessary to make a smooth elastic dough.)

3. Grease a large bowl and place the dough in it, turning it once so that the top of the dough is lightly coated in fat. Cover the bowl with a clean towel and let the dough rise until it is doubled in size, about 1½ hours.

4. Punch the dough back down and fold the dough over itself in thirds. Knead the dough back into a ball, grease, cover it again, and let it rise again until almost doubled in size, about 1½ hours more.

5. Place an empty heavy skillet on the lowest rack of the oven, and for the best results, a pizza or bread-baking stone on the middle shelf. If you don't have a baking stone, use a heavy baking sheet. Preheat the oven to 400° F.

The Life of a Horno

Hornos used to be almost as common as piñon pines in the hills and valleys of northern New Mexico, but they are not simple to build, use, or maintain against the ravages of the weather. Candido Valerio, of Los Cordovas outside of Taos, can tell you all about it. Born just a decade after statehood, he hand-built the family's adobe home, forming the bricks himself with the help of his children, and then erected a horno the same way for his late wife, Anita.

Like other cooks before and after her, Anita heated the thick walls of the horno with a wood fire, checked the temperature by holding her hand inside briefly, swept out most or all of the coals, and baked bread by placing loaves on the horno floor, like in a pizza oven.

Candido's daughter Luisa Mylet, an employee of Hacienda de los Martinez in Taos, knew her father was the right man for the job when the museum's hornos needed serious repairs in 2010. Even though Candido was approaching ninety at the time, he leaped into the task with enthusiasm. He specified that the dirt needed to come from holes of *las tuzas*, or gophers, because the gophers would have done the tough work of breaking the hard-packed clay into fine bits. Candido chopped up straw to mix with the dirt and water into a thick patching material, which he spread onto each horno with a piece of sheepskin and then let it dry in the summer sun for about two weeks. After the curing time, Candido repeated the process but with a thinner, creamier mud glaze formed with more finely chopped straw as the binder. The finished ovens cured for about two weeks before being fired up for baking.

6. Using a large spatula, transfer the dough to the heated baking stone or sheet. Before closing the oven, pour ½ cup of water into the skillet to create steam in the oven. Close the oven and immediately turn the heat down to 350° F. Bake the bread for 55 to 60 minutes. It is ready when lightly browned and crusty and sounds hollow when thumped (an internal temperature of 200° F). Cool on a baking rack. Serve slightly warm or at room temperature.

Working ahead: It's hard to speed up yeast bread, but you can slow it down to fit the process better into your schedule. At either of the recipe's rising stages, you can choose to put the covered bowl of dough in the refrigerator overnight. Let it sit for about 30 minutes at room temperature before proceeding with the recipe.

Variations: Chile-laced baking-powder-raised corn breads have been American staples for decades, but you're not likely to find green chile cheese bread outside New Mexico. Instead of forming the dough into one large round, make two cylindrical loaves, first dividing the dough and patting it down into a pair of ½-inch-thick rectangles. Mash up 1 cup of Chile Verde Table Relish (page 27) and spread half on each rectangle, leaving about ½ inch of the outer border uncovered on the dough. Scatter each with about 2 ounces of shredded medium or sharp cheddar cheese and roll up pinwheel style. Bake as above but plan on a baking time of 35 to 45 minutes.

Sopaipillas

Known affectionately sometimes as sofa pillows, these rectangular- or wedge-shaped deep-fried poofs of hot dough have a place at every traditional table. In northern New Mexico, they always come on the side as a bread with the main course, even with a starchy entree like a burrito. Served with drizzles of honey, they cut the heat of chile. The closer you get to Las Cruces in the south the more likely it becomes that the sopaipillas will be a dessert choice instead. Many people make sopaipillas out of the same dough they use for flour tortillas, perhaps with a touch of added sugar, but the deep-frying results in an entirely different bread than a griddle-cooked tortilla. We started adding a portion of whole wheat flour or sprouted wheat panocha flour (page 154) to our sopaipillas after tasting those at the sorely missed Truchas Mountain Café, owned and operated in its too-brief life by Josephine and Michael Romero.

Makes 12 sopaipillasw

1½ cups all-purpose flour

½ cup whole wheat flour

1 teaspoon salt

1 teaspoon baking powder

1 teaspoon sugar, optional

2 teaspoons vegetable oil, vegetable shortening, or lard

¼ cup milk or evaporated milk, room temperature

½ cup lukewarm water, or more as needed

vegetable oil for deep-frying

honey

1. Stir together the flours, salt, baking powder, and the optional sugar in a large bowl. Work in the oil, using clean fingers to combine. Add the milk and water, working the liquids into the flour until a sticky dough forms. Pour in a bit more water if the dough isn't sticking together as a rough shaggy mess.

2. Knead the dough on a lightly floured surface vigorously for 1 minute. The dough should be soft but feeling a bit sturdy and no longer sticky. Let the dough rest, covered with a damp cloth, for 15 minutes. Divide the dough into 3 balls, cover the balls with the damp cloth, and let them rest for another 15 to 30 minutes.

3. Roll out each ball of dough on a lightly floured surface into a circle or rectangle approximately ¼-inch thick. If you have a tortilla roller, use it rather than a heavier rolling pin, which compacts the dough more. Trim off any ragged edges and discard them. To avoid toughening the dough, try to avoid rerolling it. Cut each portion of dough into 4 wedges or smaller rectangles.

4. Heat at least 3 inches of oil in a heavy, high-sided saucepan or skillet to 400° F. Slip 1 or 2 dough pieces into the oil. After sinking briefly, the sopaipillas should begin to balloon and rise back to the surface. Once they start bobbing at the top, carefully spoon oil over them for the few seconds it will take until they have

fully puffed. Turn them over (we like a long-handled slotted spoon for this) and cook just until they are golden. Drain.

5. Arrange the sopaipillas in a napkin-lined basket and serve immediately with honey. Tear a corner off your sopaipilla to let steam escape, drizzle honey through the hole into the hollow center, and enjoy.

Working ahead: The dough can be made up to 4 hours ahead, then covered tightly and refrigerated. Let it sit at room temperature about 15 minutes before proceeding.

Variations: This is a dish that can always spark an argument. Some folks make sopaipillas with yeast dough, and others use both yeast and baking powder. Some insist upon all milk for the liquid, and some add a whole egg or a yolk for extra richness. Then there's the usual lard versus shortening versus vegetable oil debate both for the dough and the frying. And, of course, plenty of cooks would skip the whole wheat flour, replacing it with more all-purpose white flour. About the only thing people agree on is that restaurants that take the shortcut of using commercially prepared biscuit dough should be publicly humiliated. Bences Gonzales, the longtime Los Alamos Ranch School cook before the Manhattan Project famously closed down the school, was known for his delectable campfire version done in a Dutch oven situated over an outdoor wood fire. Anyone who ate his version says they were the best ever. In about the same era, Eloisa Delgado de Stewart was recommending *enmelado* as an accompaniment in place of honey. In her *El Plato Sabroso Recipes*, she put together for the syrup 1 pound of brown sugar, 1 quart of water, 1 tablespoon of lard, and 1 tablespoon of ground allspice, a mixture that was simmered in a saucepan until reduced by ¾. Cut the ingredients proportionately for smaller servings. This type of syrup was also used with *buñuelos*, fried dough rounds that are something of a cross between sopaipillas and fry bread.

Navajo Fry Bread

After their forced Long Walk in 1864 from their ancestral lands to a distant military camp, the Diné concocted fry bread out of necessity. No longer able to raise sufficient food for themselves in a new environment without their sheep and other traditional resources, they often had to rely on U.S. Army handouts, which included bags of rancid flour. To kill the bugs in the flour, they fried their dough in hot oil. The process created a now-beloved treat, a golden disk simultaneously—and wondrously—flaky, chewy, and crispy. For making fry bread today many aficionados insist on hydrogenated Morrell Snow Cap lard, and most particularly, on Blue Bird flour, a soft wheat flour in a beautiful cloth bag milled just north of New Mexico in Cortez, Colorado. If you can't find Blue Bird, at least try to get a soft wheat or biscuit flour.

Makes 6 to 8 large rounds

3 cups soft wheat pastry or biscuit flour, or all-purpose flour

1 tablespoon baking powder (reduce by ½ teaspoon at altitudes above 5,000 feet)

1 teaspoon salt

1 tablespoon milk powder, optional

approximately 1¼ cups warm water

vegetable oil, lard, or vegetable shortening, for frying

confectioners' sugar

1. Preheat the oven to 200° F.

2. Stir together the flour, baking powder, salt, and optional milk powder in a large bowl. Add the water, about ¼ cup at a time, working the liquid into the flour with your fingers. The dough will be sticky at first. Keep working it until it becomes soft and pliable and no longer sticks to your fingers or the bowl.

3. Knead the dough on a flour-covered surface for several minutes. Work from the outer edges into the center as you knead. Let the dough rest, covered with a damp cloth, for 15 minutes.

The Virtues of Isolation

Both Spain and the United States found that New Mexico was mostly unsettleable, at least with preindustrial technologies. The arable lands of the territory consisted almost exclusively of narrow river and stream valleys and were too few and too widely scattered to allow the growth of large agricultural populations. Instead the landscape produced a dispersed pattern of settlement consisting of many small enclaves of population and culture. These mostly Pueblo and Hispano villages became bastions of cultural preservation, for they were at once so self-sufficient that they had little need for the outside world and yet so poor that the outside world had little need of them. In isolation they persisted for centuries, changing little.

—WILLIAM DEBUYS, *ENCHANTMENT AND EXPLOITATION: THE LIFE AND HARD TIMES OF A NEW MEXICO MOUNTAIN RANGE* (1985)

4. Form the dough into 6 or 8 balls. Let them sit for 5 to 10 minutes, then pat and push each ball down into a ½-inch-thick disk. Take the first dough disk in your hands and stretch it into a pizza-dough-like round of 9 to 10 inches. If you wish, poke a small hole in the center of the dough, a vestige from the days when the breads were turned in the fryer with a stick. Our dough often seems to get a hole in it from our handling of it so we usually don't make one in its center on purpose. Repeat with the remaining dough balls. If you need to stack the rounds to have room for the whole batch, place wax paper between them.

5. Pour about 1 inch of oil (or melt enough lard) into a heavy, high-sided saucepan or skillet. Warm the oil over medium heat until it is shimmering but not smoking. Carefully transfer a round to the oil. Fry for 1 to 2 minutes, until puffed and lightly golden. Flip the bread (we like an oversize fork for this) and cook 1 or 2 minutes, until golden. Drain on paper towels. Place in the oven on a baking sheet and cover with a clean dish towel. Repeat the cooking process with the remaining fry breads and keep them warm in the oven until all are ready. (Once you are skilled, you can fry the first bread while forming the second, and so on.)

6. The side of each fry bread that was cooked first will have more of the desirable uneven bubbles than the second. Dust the more nubbly, bubbly side of each with confectioners' sugar and serve right away.

Variations: Fry bread is frequently served with a sprinkling of cinnamon sugar or a smear of honey instead of powdered sugar. It can also be eaten in a more savory style, with salt or garlic salt. Whether sweet or savory, ground sunflower-seed kernels, ground or whole, can be sprinkled over the top just as it comes out of the hot oil.

Sweet Anise Molletes

In the era when most people made their own bread, home bakers would have a standard simple bread or biscuit dough and when circumstance and availability allowed they would enrich that dough with eggs, fat, milk, sugar, or spices. This bun, scented with *aniz* (anise), became a standard here, much as cinnamon rolls did in other American areas. Different Hispano cultures make rolls similar to this that go by a variety of names, including *bollete* and *semita*, and the term "mollete" is often used in other places to describe any baked roll.

Makes about 1 dozen

Rolls

¾ cup milk or goat milk

3 tablespoons unsalted butter, plus more for greasing the bowl

3 tablespoons lard or vegetable shortening

½ cup sugar

½ teaspoon salt

2 large eggs, lightly beaten

3 cups sifted all-purpose flour, or more as needed

1 package (¼ ounce) rapid-rise yeast

2 tablespoons anise seeds, toasted in a dry skillet and ground

Topping

¼ cup sugar

1 teaspoon anise seeds, toasted and ground

3 tablespoons unsalted butter, melted

For rolls

1. Warm the milk with the butter and shortening in a small saucepan until the fats are melted. Pour the milk mixture into the bowl of a large sturdy mixer equipped with a dough hook and stir in the sugar and salt. Cool to lukewarm. Start the mixer on medium speed and mix in the eggs. Stir together the 3 cups of flour, yeast, and anise and add them about ⅓ at a time to the mixer. Stop the mixer, if needed, to scrape down the bowl's sides. Beat for about 5 minutes, or until the dough becomes smooth and satiny. It should remain a little sticky, but if it is gluey—more like batter than dough—it needs a little more flour beaten in. Remove dough from the mixer bowl and form into a ball. (Alternatively, the dough can be mixed by hand and kneaded for about 10 minutes on a lightly floured surface.)

Major General Charles H. Corlett, a hero of Pacific campaigns during World War II, lived during peacetime on a ranch near the collapsed Jemez Mountain volcano crater now known as the Valles Caldera National Preserve. Called "Cowboy Pete" by friends, he contributed the following instructions for cowboy biscuits to the Española Hospital Auxiliary's *Española Valley Cookbook* (1975).

"All you need to make biscuits is a sack of flour, baking powder, salt, a little lard or bear grease, a little canned milk, or water will do, a Dutch oven, on a fire burning down to coals. First, lean your sack of flour against a stump. Then go to the creek and wash your hands good. Come back to the flour, open the sack, after you shake it down, roll the top back all around without spilling any flour. Make a little hole in the top of the flour. Put into the hole a good sized pinch of baking powder and salt, a small handful of lard or grease, and mix it all up, shallow like, while it is dry. Then put in the hole just enough canned milk or water to make a nice lump of dough. Pull the dough out and work it a little with your hands. If you have a bacon rind, wipe it around the inside of the hot Dutch oven. Then pull off bits of dough and shape them in nice biscuit size lumps and put them in the Dutch oven. Fit the top on the oven and cover it with hot coals. Leave it ten minutes. Open up the oven and yell 'Come and get it.' "

2. Rinse and dry the mixer bowl, then coat the inside lightly with butter. Place the dough back in the bowl, turning it over so that all sides have a film of butter. Cover the bowl loosely with a clean dish towel and set it aside in a warm place until the dough rises to double its original size, about 1½ hours. Punch down the dough, knead it several times, and cover it once more. Let it rise again until doubled in size, about 1½ hours more.

3. Divide the dough into balls about twice the size of a golf ball. Flatten each ball with your palm, a tortilla roller, or a rolling pin to a disk about ½ inch in thickness and 3 inches across. Transfer the dough disks to a greased baking sheet, spacing them about 1 inch apart.

For topping

1. Combine the sugar and anise in a small bowl.

Assembly

1. Brush the rolls with about half of the melted butter and sprinkle them with the topping. Let them sit until nearly doubled, about 1 hour.

2. Meanwhile, preheat the oven to 375° F.

3. Bake for 18 to 20 minutes, until the rolls are raised and golden brown. Brush tops with the remaining melted butter. Serve warm.

Working ahead: To have molletes for breakfast, with minimal prep time that morning, use one of two techniques. Cover the assembled buns with the towel and place them in the refrigerator to rise slowly overnight. Let them sit out at room temperature before baking for about 20 minutes while the oven preheats. Otherwise, you can choose to bake the molletes the evening before, let them cool, and then cover them tightly with plastic. In the morning, rewrap them in foil and reheat in a 250° F oven for about 15 minutes.

Variations: New Mexican azafrán can also be added to the dough for a sunny golden hue. Add 1 teaspoon of it to the milk and fat when heating so that it will color the dough evenly. If you're a big fan of cinnamon rolls, add a teaspoon of ground cinnamon to the topping before sprinkling it over the rolls.

Pumpkin Piñon Bread

Pueblo and Diné cooks use pumpkin in all manner of quick breads as well as in cookies and cakes. This dish was contributed by our friend and colleague Lois Ellen Frank, author of the James Beard Award—winning cookbook *Foods of the Southwest Indian Nations*, where this recipe first appeared. Lois has a doctorate in cultural anthropology from the University of New Mexico, with a focus on Native American food and plants. Her bread, lightly sweet and quite moist, can be served as a snack or toasted at breakfast. Lois's Red Mesa Cuisine business, owned jointly with Walter Whitewater, sometimes serves the bread as the basis of a dessert, topped with pumpkin sauce and pumpkin ice cream.

Makes 2 loaves

2 cups all-purpose flour

1 teaspoon baking soda (reduce by ⅛ teaspoon at altitudes above 5,000 feet)

½ teaspoon salt

1½ cups sugar

2 teaspoons ground cinnamon

3 large eggs, beaten

¾ cup milk

½ cup sunflower oil, preferably, or canola oil

1 teaspoon pure vanilla extract

2 cups pumpkin puree (canned or homemade as described in the accompanying tip)

1 cup piñon nuts, toasted in a dry skillet

1. Preheat the oven to 350° F. Grease 2 9-inch loaf pans.

2. Sift together the flour, baking soda, salt, sugar, and cinnamon.

3. In another bowl combine the eggs, milk, oil, and vanilla, and mix well. Stir in the pumpkin puree and the dry ingredients, mix well, then fold in the piñons.

4. Pour the batter into the prepared pans. Bake for approximately 45 minutes, until the bread springs back when touched.

5. Cool briefly, then run a knife around the inside of each pan and turn the loaves out on a baking rack. Turn over the loaves so that the top sides cool facing up. Slice and serve warm or cool.

Working ahead: The bread will keep for several days if tightly wrapped. Toast it after the first day for best flavor.

TIP

How to Make Your Own Pumpkin Puree

• Select a pumpkin of about 2 to 2½ pounds, grown for flavor, not for jack-o'-lantern looks. A cheese pumpkin or an Acoma squash or other Pueblo winter squash can be used.

• Cut off the stem and slice the pumpkin into 4 or 6 wedges. Scoop out the seeds and stringy pulp.

• Place wedges on a baking sheet and bake in a 350° F oven for about 45 minutes or until soft.

• When cool enough to handle, scoop pumpkin meat away from the skins and puree the pumpkin in a food processor. Remove any fibrous strings that remain. You should have about 2 cups of pumpkin puree. The pumpkin is ready to use, but it can be refrigerated in a nonreactive bowl for a few days or frozen for several months.

9 Desserts

The early Spanish colonists brought sweet-food traditions with them to New Mexico from the mother country and even the ancient Middle East, but they rarely ate desserts as the final course of a meal. They generally saved the scarce supplies of sugar, honey, and spices for holidays and fiestas, though affluent families relished sweet nibbles when feasible at afternoon teas called *meriendas*. Puebloans largely lacked experience with sweet foods and the whole notion of desserts, but they welcomed the Spanish introduction of fruit trees.

Among desserts with widespread popularity today, flan and natillas have deep roots in southern Spain. Sherry producers of centuries ago used egg whites to clarify their fortified wine and gave the leftover yolks to nearby convents, where nuns developed an array of applications that included rich custards. Capirotada, another local favorite, goes further back in time, at least to the early Western civilizations that made old bread good again as a pudding.

Hispano settlers imported chocolate from Mexico, where it originated, but never made desserts with it. As in Europe in the same period, people drank chocolate as a hot beverage and didn't eat it in other ways. It did become extremely popular as a dessert in New Mexico, like elsewhere, in the twentieth century. In recognition of this, we wrap up the chapter with the most famous chocolate cake ever made in the state.

Biscochitos

If you harbor any doubts at all about the New Mexican reverence for traditional foods, consider this. Back in the 1980s, our legislature was the first in the country to designate a state cookie, though the decision was fraught with discord. Apparently, according to accounts, no one objected to the notion of a state cookie, and everyone agreed on the cookie to be anointed. The divisive debate focused on the spelling of the name, whether the third letter should be "s" or "z." *Bizcochito* won out in the legislature but most people continued to spell it with "s." And if that's not troublesome enough, in the southern end of the state lots of folks call the cookie a *biscocho*. By whatever name, these anise-scented, lard-enriched shortbreads are essential to weddings, graduations, and anniversaries, and are so popular at Christmas that food writer Chichi Wang, who grew up in Los Alamos, says, "In December, biscochitos comprise maybe thirty percent of the diet of the average New Mexican." This version, which first appeared in our book *American Home Cooking* (1999), is so good it bears repeating here. The recipe originated with Lydia Garcia, the mother of our friend Dorothy Montaño. Dorothy made a minor variation from Lydia's original, which has had the whole family talking about the merits of each for years since. Unless you're cooking for vegetarians, don't substitute any other fat for the lard, which is essential to the taste and flaky texture. A great biscochito should melt in your mouth, and that requires a generous amount of vigorous whipping to aerate the lard-and-sugar base, and then takes a light hand in the handling of the dough. Historically, these are often formed by hand into a fleur-de-lis shape. Despite the symbol's common identification with France, it also represents the Kingdom of Spain and the Spanish monarchy's connection to the House of Bourbon.

Makes about 48 medium-size cookies

Cookies

3 cups unbleached all-purpose flour

1½ teaspoons baking powder (reduce by ¼ teaspoon at altitudes above 5,000 feet)

1 to 1½ teaspoons ground anise

½ teaspoon salt

½ pound lard, softened

½ cup plus 1 tablespoon sugar

1 large egg

2 tablespoons sweet white wine, brandy, or rum, or apple or pineapple juice

Topping

¼ cup sugar

¾ teaspoon ground cinnamon

Lard Almighty

There are so many things I love about where I live. One of them is those cultural givens that we take for granted, like Morrell lard. Las Cruces, New Mexico, is one of the few places that I've lived that has a run on Morrell lard each Christmas and at various other times throughout the year. I have driven across town and back again, in desperation, all hours of the day and night, searching for lard. Many of you have probably suffered the same fate. Lard is as necessary to us as air. There is no way you can make the perfect biscocho, our beloved sugar cookies—and I've tried—without lard.

—DENISE CHÁVEZ, *A TACO TESTIMONY* (2006)

For the cookies

1. Sift together the flour, baking powder, anise, and salt.

2. Beat the lard in an electric mixer, gradually adding the sugar, until extremely fluffy and light, about 8 minutes. Don't shortcut this step. Stop the mixer every couple of minutes and scrape the sides of the mixing bowl. Add the egg, followed by the wine, and continue beating. Mix in the dry ingredients, adding about ⅓ of the mixture at a time. Stop the mixer as you make each addition and beat no longer than necessary to incorporate the dry ingredients. A stiff pie-crust-type dough is what you're seeking. Chill the dough for about 15 minutes for easy handling.

3. Preheat the oven to 350° F.

4. Dorothy uses a cookie press to form her biscochitos, choosing a customary fleur-de-lis design. If you don't own a cookie press, the dough can be rolled out ¼-inch thick on a floured work surface and cut with a paring knife into fleurs-de-lis or cut with a small cookie cutter, often a diamond shape. Avoid handling the dough any more than necessary, one of the keys to the melt-in-your-mouth texture. Transfer the cookies to ungreased cookie sheets.

5. Bake the cookies for 10 to 12 minutes, until just set and pale golden.

For the topping

1. While the cookies bake, stir together the topping ingredients.

Assembly

1. When the cookies are done, cool for just 1 or 2 minutes on the baking sheets, then gently dunk the top of each in the cinnamon-sugar. Transfer to baking racks to finish cooling. In a New Mexican household, about half of the cookies will disappear before they are cool. Consider yourself warned.

Working ahead: Biscochitos, tightly covered, will keep for at least a week. They also freeze well for up to a month.

Variations: Pat Felhauer was a relatively new resident to Las Cruces when she saw information in 2007 about a Blue Bell ice-cream flavor competition in neighboring Texas. Pat and her husband had already come to love the local biscochitos and the pecans that grow so profusely near the Rio Grande, so she created for the contest Pecan Biscochito Grande Ice Cream. In the end, Blue Bell chose another flavor, perhaps not wanting to highlight something with such strong roots in the state next door. Blue Bell gave the Felhauers permission to suggest in print this simple version, one New Mexicans will recognize as a winner. Soften a half-gallon of Blue Bell premium vanilla ice cream or other premium vanilla ice cream in its carton for 20 minutes at room temperature. Spoon it into a large mixing bowl or an ice-cream maker, saving the carton. Mix in 1 cup of biscochito cookies cut into ½-inch pieces and 1 cup of chopped pecans. If mixing by hand, stir all of the ingredients together until well combined. If using an ice-cream maker, follow the manufacturer's directions. Return the ice cream with the mix-ins to the original carton. Refreeze to firm up, then enjoy.

Capirotada

New Mexicans make a variety of bread puddings called capirotada, *torrejas*, or *sopa*, as in *sopa seca*, a dish made with liquid that absorbs during cooking. Because of the religious symbolism of bread, the dessert is often associated with Lent or served for Easter dinner. This syrup-soaked bread pudding always surprises diners who have sampled only the cream-and-egg-enriched versions evolved from French tradition; both are good but quite different in taste. Capirotada is typically made with a horno-style baked loaf, but it can also be made with any other white bread.

Serves 8

½ cup raisins

⅓ cup brandy

1 pound basic store-bought white bread, or Horno-Style Bread (page 140), torn into bite-size pieces

2 cups sugar

2½ cups hot water

1 cup pear nectar or water

6 tablespoons unsalted butter

2 teaspoons pure vanilla extract

1 teaspoon ground *canela* (Mexican cinnamon) or other cinnamon

pinch of ground cloves, optional

1 ripe pear, peeled and chopped, optional

½ cup chopped pecans, toasted

1½ cups (6 ounces) shredded Colby, mild cheddar, or Monterey Jack cheese

softly whipped cream, optional

1. Preheat the oven to 350° F. Butter a 9 by 12 baking dish.

2. Place the bread on a baking sheet and bake about 20 minutes, until lightly crisp and golden.

3. Meanwhile, place the raisins in a small bowl and pour the brandy over them. Set aside to soften.

4. Pour the sugar into a large heavy saucepan. Warm it over medium-high heat until the sugar melts and turns a deep golden brown, about 8 to 10 minutes. Stir occasionally to assure even melting. Pour the water into the molten sugar, standing back from the pan to avoid the steam that will rise as the water hits the sugar. The syrup mixture will partially solidify. Continue cooking until it becomes liquid again, stirring occasionally. Add the pear nectar, butter, vanilla, and spices to the syrup.

5. Dump half of the bread into the baking dish. Scatter with half of the optional pear, pecans, cheese, and raisins. Repeat with the remaining bread, pear, pecans, cheese, and raisins, including any brandy not absorbed by the fruit, and push everything down into the bread just a bit.

6. Ladle the syrup slowly over the bread mixture. The syrup should be about level with the top of the bread. If any bread pieces aren't coated, push them into the syrup.

7. Bake for 20 to 25 minutes, until the syrup has absorbed, the cheese has melted, and some of the top bits are crusty. Serve the pudding hot, topped with whipped cream if you like.

Variations: New Mexico's most abundant fruits, apples and apricots (chopped dried or fresh), sometimes enhance capirotada to scrumptious effect. Sauté either of them in a little butter before adding to the pudding in place of the pear, which is already soft enough without precooking. Replace the pear nectar with apple cider. A little New Mexican azafrán can also be mixed into the syrup, a lovely touch. You don't see this much anymore, but some cooks used to deep-fry the bread for the pudding or add tomatoes and sometimes even onion.

Panocha

This simple improvised creation, a colonial frontier "make-do" dish, is still beloved in New Mexico. When processed sugar wasn't available and honey was too scarce to use regularly, Spanish settlers converted wheat starch to sugar by sprouting some of the wheat berries in a wet bag placed in a warm spot before grinding the rest of the grain into flour. After long cooking with water, the flour turned into a dark brown pudding they called panocha. Cooks today add sugar and a variety of enrichments that can include vanilla, ginger, or raisins in addition to those featured below. Loida Ortiz, once a cook at Rancho de Chimayó Restaurante, first taught us how to make the dish. Commercial panocha flour is most readily available in the late winter and early spring because the dessert is commonly served during Lent and at Easter (see New Mexico Culinary Resources, page 187). In her 1939 cookbook *The Genuine New Mexico Tasty Recipes*, Cleofas M. Jaramillo talks about special Easter desserts: "There was a great deal of exchanging done of *charolitas*—dishes—at noon on both Holy Thursday and Good Friday. Neighbors and friends were seen carrying back and forth small bowls filled with panocha, capirotada, *torejas*, or whatever other nice dish they had prepared. This exchange went on in every small village during Holy Week."

Serves 8 to 12

15-ounce package (about 2½ cups) harina para panocha (panocha flour)

1¼ cups all-purpose flour

4½ cups water

½ cup molasses, sorghum, or packed dark brown sugar

2 tablespoons unsalted butter, plus more for greasing the baking dish

1 teaspoon salt

1 teaspoon ground cinnamon or ½ teaspoon ground nutmeg

½ cup milk

softly whipped cream or vanilla ice cream, optional

Cleofas Martinez Jaramillo, 1878–1956

Born in Arroyo Hondo into one of the wealthiest land-grant families in New Mexico, Cleofas Martinez attended boarding schools in Taos and Santa Fe run by the Sisters of Loretto. As a student in Santa Fe, she won the heart of a rising territorial official, Venceslao Jaramillo, her cousin. The couple got married in a glamorous Taos ceremony in 1898, honeymooned in California, and went to live in the groom's hometown of El Rito, near his 33,000-acre sheep ranch.

Tragedy soon overtook the family. The Jaramillos' first two children died in infancy, and the only surviving daughter was murdered at the age of eighteen. Venceslao died early as well, just a few months before he was scheduled to serve as a delegate to the 1920 Republican National Convention.

Cleofas devoted the remaining years of her life to cultural preservation in the state. In 1935 she inspired the founding of La Sociedad Folklórica and became a prolific writer over the next two decades, documenting New Mexico folktales, customs, and religious ceremonies. Her 1939 cookbook *The Genuine New Mexico Tasty Recipes*, remains one of the state's culinary classics.

1. Sift the panocha flour. Up to a few teaspoons of it will likely be too coarse for sifting. Discard any quantity that remains in the sifter. Then sift the panocha flour and all-purpose flour together into a large heavy saucepan.

2. In a second smaller saucepan, bring the water to a boil. Stir in the molasses (or sorghum or brown sugar), butter, salt, and cinnamon (or nutmeg). When the molasses and butter have melted into the liquid, pour about 1 cup at a time into the flour and stir until smooth. The batter will resemble Cream of Wheat cereal. Let it sit for about 15 minutes.

3. While the batter sits, preheat the oven to 300° F. Butter a large baking dish.

4. Bring the batter to a boil over medium heat. Reduce the heat to a simmer and cook for 20 minutes, stirring frequently. The texture of the pudding changes during cooking from grainy to somewhat silky, and the color deepens. It will be sticky. Remove from the stove and stir in the milk.

5. Scrape the batter into the prepared baking dish. Bake a total of 2 to 2¼ hours, until it's cooked down by about ¼, pudding-like in texture, very brown, and a bit glossy. Check after about 1½ hours and cover with foil if it is starting to look dry.

6. Serve warm, spooned into bowls. Cream or ice cream makes a welcome cooling accompaniment if you wish.

Working ahead: Panocha can be made through the stovetop cooking step and spooned into the baking dish to cover and refrigerate overnight. Bring back to cool room temperature the next day to bake. Alternatively, the entire dish can be made ahead and refrigerated for a week. Reheat covered in a low-heat oven before serving.

Flan

Still popular in Spain and most of its former colonies, creamy, silky flan makes a cooling finish to a spicy New Mexican meal. Its light firmness should come from egg yolks rather than the gelatin sometimes employed in warm climates. Flan's prominence among local desserts emerged in an era before regular refrigeration, when canned milk products were a huge convenience item. Even though it's much easier today to find fresh milk or cream, many New Mexicans prefer the familiar taste of their mother's or grandmother's recipe that relied on evaporated or sweetened condensed milk.

Serves 6 to 8

Caramel

½ cup granulated sugar

Custard

2 cups whole milk or goat milk	3 large eggs
14-ounce can sweetened condensed milk	4 large egg yolks
	1½ teaspoons pure vanilla extract

For caramel

1. Have 6 or 8 ¾- to 1-cup heatproof ramekins or baking cups near the stovetop.

2. Pour the sugar into a small heavy saucepan or skillet. Cook over low heat, watching as the sugar melts into a golden brown caramel syrup. Don't stir unless the sugar melts unevenly. When the syrup turns a rich medium brown, immediately remove the pan from the heat and carefully pour about 1 tablespoon into each ramekin. The syrup will harden almost immediately.

For custard

1. Preheat the oven to 300° F.

2. Combine the ingredients in a large heavy saucepan, then whisk until the custard mixture is well blended and frothy. Heat the custard over medium-low heat until it is just warm throughout; do not let it boil. Divide the custard among the ramekins.

3. Set ramekins in a roasting pan or other large baking pan. Make a water bath for the cups, pouring hot water into the baking dish to a depth of about 1 inch. Bake about 1 hour and 10 minutes, until the flan is barely firm. The tops may have colored lightly. Remove from the oven and let the flan cool about 20 minutes in the hot-water bath. Remove ramekins from the roasting pan, discarding the water.

4. Cover the ramekins and refrigerate for at least 3 hours.

5. To unmold the flan, run a knife between the edge of each flan and ramekin. Invert each onto a dessert plate, letting caramel run down the sides. Serve cool.

Working ahead: Flan can be made up to two days ahead. Refrigerate in the original cups and unmold shortly before serving time.

Variations: The flan can be made in a round 2-quart baking dish rather than in individual ramekins. Add about 15 minutes to the baking time and at least 1 more hour to the chilling time. Whatever the size and shape of the flan, a few fresh peach or apricot slices are a nice accompaniment in season.

Natillas

Another locally adored custard, natillas—or "Taos pudding," as some cooks call it—isn't as rich or dense as flan. Cooked stovetop, it often gets lightened "floating island" style with whipped egg whites. We like to add a few Mora raspberries or a drizzle of raspberry jam to brighten each serving.

Serves 6 to 8

1 quart half-and-half (divided use)

¾ cup sugar (divided use)

dash of salt

4 large eggs

2 tablespoons cornstarch

1 teaspoon pure vanilla extract

1. Combine ¾ of the half-and-half, ½ cup plus 2 tablespoons of the sugar, and the salt in a medium saucepan and warm over medium heat, stirring enough for the sugar to dissolve.

2. Meanwhile, separate the eggs. Place the whites in a mixing bowl. Whisk together the egg yolks and the remaining half-and-half in a smaller bowl, then sprinkle the cornstarch over the egg yolk mixture and whisk again.

3. Once the half-and-half and sugar mixture comes just to a boil, remove the pan from the heat. Pour the egg yolk mixture through a strainer into the saucepan and immediately whisk the combined mixture well. Return the saucepan to the stove and continue cooking over medium heat, stirring often. Cook another 5 to 8 minutes until the mixture has thickened enough to coat the back of a spoon. Remove from the heat and stir in the vanilla.

4. Beat the egg whites with the remaining 2 tablespoons of sugar until soft peaks form. Fold the beaten egg whites into the custard, leaving the whites a bit peaky in spots. Serve the natillas warm or chilled.

Variations: Philomena Romero founded and ran Philomena's, a restaurant once located on the site of the Manhattan Project's guardhouse in Los Alamos, and in 1970 wrote a cookbook, *New Mexican Dishes*. She combined two popular desserts, natillas and rice pudding, into one. She started by making natillas and then folded into it 1 cup of cooked rice, ½ cup of crushed pineapple, and ¼ cup of raisins.

Rice Pudding and Remembrance

Maria Lucia Trujillo, a Santa Fe native, shared with us this loving remembrance of her mother and her cinnamon-dusted rice pudding.

"She was born in northern New Mexico on the first day of spring, 1912. Her name was Lucaria Trujillo, but she chose to be called Carrie. She was strong, stubborn, and her distinctive sense of style was way ahead of her time. Rice pudding recipes are fairly ordinary, I know, but what made my mother's recipe unique and memorable is the standard she set for presentation: 'Always serve rice pudding in a pretty bowl.' I was so influenced by the importance she placed not only on preparing the best food but on understanding that it somehow tastes better if it's dressed better. She cooked the way she looked. Pretty."

Cajeta de Membrillo

Fruit conserves—from jams and jellies to this slow-cooked quince dessert paste—have long been a part of New Mexico larders. Our recipe comes from Reynalda Ortiz y Piño de Dinkel—Mrs. Dinkel to the numerous Santa Feans to whom she taught Spanish in the local schools over three decades. Reynalda was born the day before New Mexico became a state, in the village of Galisteo, into one of the state's most recognized and influential families. She was a tireless promoter and researcher of New Mexico's ties to Spain and, at the time of her death in 1997, was the last founding member of La Sociedad Folklórica. Reynalda served her membrillo, which first appeared in *La Herencia* magazine, in the quintessential Spanish manner, with Manchego cheese. Since the quinces she used came directly off of the tree, her directions began with, "Remove the fuzz from the quince with a Chore-girl."

Serves 8 or more

8 large quinces

water

about 4 cups sugar

1. Slice each quince into 8 pieces. (No need to peel or core the fruit.) Put the pieces into a large saucepan and cover with water to the top of the fruit. Simmer over medium-low heat until soft, about 45 minutes. Much of the water will have evaporated.

2. Preheat the oven to 250° F.

3. Put the fruit through a food mill to puree it, which will leave the skins and cores behind. Measure the quince puree and spoon it into a lightly oiled 9 by 13 baking pan. Add 1 cup of sugar per 1 cup of quince puree and stir. Bake for about 4 hours total, stirring up from the bottom and scraping down the dish's sides after about 2 hours. Continue baking for about 2 hours more, until the membrillo has darkened considerably in color and looks like very thick jam (it should only jiggle slightly).

4. Set aside to cool, then cover and refrigerate. (It will gel further as it cools.) Once gelled fully, run a knife around the inside of the dish, turn the dish upside down, and unmold the membrillo onto a work surface or plate. Slice about ½-inch thick. Alternatively, if the mixture is too soft to slice, simply spoon it out as you would jam. Serve with cheese, preferably a tangy sheep or goat cheese.

Working ahead: Since making cajeta de membrillo was a way to preserve the fruit for long storage, it keeps quite well. Refrigerate it, tightly covered, and it will stay delicious for weeks.

Variations: If the long baking required to cook quinces down to membrillo seems like too great a time commitment, make quince butter instead. After putting the fruit through the food mill as in the recipe, return the quince puree to the pan. Add 1 cup of sugar and, if you wish, the juice of an orange. Simmer over medium-low heat until jammy. Pour into sterilized jars, cool, and refrigerate. The quince butter will keep for several weeks.

Sweetmeat Empanaditas

Half-moon fried mincemeat pastries nearly bursting with filling, these empanaditas reach the height of popularity around Christmas, just like biscochitos. No matter what their size, and whether they are served as a snack or dessert, many New Mexicans call them by the diminutive name ending in "ita" rather than empanada. As with tamales, it's best to have a group of cooks on hand to handle the multiple tasks involved with the holiday treats. Kids love crimping the dough and are thrilled when any fall apart in the fryer, meaning they get to eat the extra-crispy, almost blackened fruity bits. This version was inspired directly by Lisa Valdez Bonney, who grew up in Cebolla, in the high country of northwest New Mexico not far from the Colorado border. She volunteers her time now as a docent at the Palace of the Governors, bringing cherished traditions to life for visitors. Lisa took a December morning to show Cheryl her annual preparation ritual, learned from her mother, who also made large batches annually. Lisa always uses the natural pork from one of the Keller's Farm Stores in Albuquerque to make her mincemeat filling.

Makes approximately 48

Filling

4 pounds pork loin, cut in 4 more or less equal pieces

salt

pepper

1 tablespoon lard, shortening, or vegetable oil

15-ounce can pumpkin puree (not pumpkin pie filling) or 2 cups homemade pumpkin puree (page 148)

1½ cups granulated sugar

2 teaspoons pure vanilla extract

1 tablespoon ground cinnamon

1 teaspoon freshly grated nutmeg

¼ teaspoon ground cloves

6-ounce package dried peaches, diced fine

1 cup raisins

1 cup piñon nuts

Dough

6 cups all-purpose flour

1½ teaspoons (½ package) rapid-rise yeast

1½ tablespoons granulated sugar

1½ tablespoons salt

¼ cup lard or vegetable shortening (do not substitute vegetable oil)

1¾ cups lukewarm water, or more as needed

lard or vegetable shortening for deep-frying

confectioners' sugar

For the filling

1. Salt and pepper the pork pieces generously.

2. Warm the lard in a large heavy pan over medium-high heat. Brown the pork, then pour over it just enough water to cover. Bring to a simmer, then cover, reduce the heat to medium low and cook until the pork is quite tender, about 1½ hours.

3. When cool enough to handle, remove the pork from the liquid, pulling off and discarding any fat. Shred the pork into bits with a food processor or a combination of your fingers and a fork.

4. Combine the pork in a bowl with the pumpkin puree, sugar, vanilla, and spices. Fold in the peaches, raisins, and piñon nuts and mix well.

For the dough

1. In a large mixing bowl, stir together the flour, yeast, sugar, and salt. Work the lard or shortening into the dry ingredients with your fingers, mixing it well. Add lukewarm water, about ½ cup at a time, as needed to make a soft, pliable dough. Cover the bowl with a clean dish towel, and let the dough rise until double in size, 1 to 1½ hours.

2. Roll the dough out into golf-ball-size spheres, 12 or so at a time, on a floured surface. Flatten a dough ball with your palm, then use a tortilla roller (or larger rolling pin) to roll it into a thin round, about 4 inches in diameter. Repeat with the remaining dough.

Assembly

1. Spoon about 1 tablespoon of filling into the center of a dough round. Fold half of the dough over to make a half-moon empanadita. Crimp the edges, either with your fingers or the tines of a fork. You may need to rub a bit of water around the outside edge of the dough to get a good seal. Repeat with the remaining dough rounds and filling.

2. Warm the lard in a large high-sided skillet or Dutch oven to 325° F. Slip a few empanaditas at a time into the skillet and fry until golden brown. Drain on paper towels. Repeat with the remaining empanaditas. Dust with confectioner's sugar while warm.

3. Serve warm or at room temperature.

Working ahead: It's often simpler to make the filling a day or even two in advance of when you plan to make the dough and finish the empanaditas. You can also form them earlier in the day and then fry them shortly before you want to serve them. While they are sublime when still warm, they can be kept for several days at room temperature if they happen to last that long.

Variations: Some New Mexicans and Hispano cooks elsewhere prefer empanaditas filled with fruit alone, but the holiday custom in the state tends to feature the sweetmeat version. The empanaditas in this recipe are similar to ones made by the Atencio family, owners of El Paragua in Española, during the Christmas season. The Atencios, though, use beef rather than pork in the mincemeat. Some folks mix meats, perhaps beef tongue and pork. The shredded meat from a roasted pig's head used to be common. Applesauce is sometimes substituted for pumpkin puree, both of which add moistness. Sometimes dark corn syrup replaces the fruit and sugar, lending its own type of moistness. Other cooks might use port or another sweet wine, along with sugar, to enhance the sweetness. A friend from northeast New Mexico looked at our recipe and commented that nutmeg and cloves were never used by his family.

Feast Day Fruit Pies

Tweety and Norm Suazo and their son Travis and his wife, Sasheen, have welcomed us warmly into their Acoma Pueblo home for Acoma Feast Day as well as Christmas dances. We look forward to Tweety's famous Pueblo fruit pies, as light and flaky as any we've tasted and filled with a delicious mixture of dried apricots and plums. When the Acoma *cacique*, or governing council, chose its new governor in early 2011, the Suazos invited us to come to their other residence, on a hilltop in Rio Rancho, where Tweety was making all the pies for the Governor's Feast. We learned how to make the pies firsthand, with Cheryl measuring Tweety's handfuls, since she made them as her mother had made them, just learning by sight what quantities of everything were needed. Like many Native American bakers, Tweety opts for Blue Bird flour, milled in Cortez, Colorado (www.cortezmilling.com), but sold widely near the pueblos and Diné reservation. Tweety says that she rolls the dough a good bit thinner than is typical at Kewa (Santo Domingo) and San Felipe. While her mother would make larger round pies, Tweety shapes hers to fit on full baking sheets since she is often transporting them to various events.

Makes 2 large baking sheets of pie squares

Filling
12 ounces dried plums

12 ounces dried apricots

water

½ to ¾ cup sugar

Topping
½ cup sugar

1 teaspoon ground cinnamon

Dough
5 cups soft wheat pastry or
  biscuit flour, or all-purpose
  flour

2 teaspoons salt

1½ teaspoons baking powder
  (reduce by ¼ teaspoon at
  altitudes above 5,000 feet)

2 cups lard or vegetable
  shortening

1¾ to 2 cups water

For the filling
1. Combine plums and apricots in a saucepan with enough water to cover them. Bring to a simmer over medium heat and cook about 25 minutes, until very soft. Most of the water will have evaporated or have been absorbed by the fruit.

2. Scrape fruit, in batches if necessary, into a food processor with the sugar. Puree.

For the topping
1. Stir together the ingredients in a small bowl.

For the dough

1. Stir together in a large bowl the flour, salt, and baking powder. Work in the lard or shortening with your fingers until evenly mixed. Add 1¾ cups water and work with your fingers to combine it. Add more water if needed to make a smooth, pie-crust–like dough. Form the dough into 4 equal-size balls.

Assembly

1. Preheat the oven to 375° F.

2. Roll out the first ball of dough on a lightly floured surface with a rolling pin into a rectangle that will fit the baking sheets, about ¼ inch in thickness. Pick the dough up carefully, winding it around the rolling pin to help support it as you tuck it onto the baking sheet, covering it fully. Spread the dough with half of the filling. Roll out the second ball of dough and place it over the filling. Crimp the outer edges neatly. Repeat with the remaining dough and filling.

3. With a pizza cutter, slice the full baking sheets of pies into squares of the size you wish. For feast days, Tweety cuts hers into squares of about 2 inches. Prick the top of each pie square with the tines of a fork, then sprinkle all lightly with the topping.

4. Bake each sheet of pie squares for about 15 minutes, reversing the position of the baking sheets on the oven racks and turning the sheets around once halfway through the baking time. Crusts should be golden brown.

5. Let pies cool on the baking sheets for about 10 minutes. Recut the squares with the pizza cutter and remove to baking racks. Eat a few warm and the rest at room temperature.

Pecan Oat Pie

The most legendary American-style pie in New Mexico is probably the apple pie with a buttery hard sauce served at Santa Fe's Pink Adobe restaurant for more than half a century. The most legendary place to eat pie, though, is Pie Town, a hamlet sitting high on the Continental Divide in west-central New Mexico's Catron County. The town moniker started as a nickname back in the 1920s, when the first in a series of pie bakers settled there, but it stuck officially once the U.S. Postal Service came to town. When Kathy Knapp passed through in 1995 looking for pie, no one was upholding the baking tradition. She chose to stay and opened the Pie-O-Neer Café, so popular now that folks often refer to Highway 60 through town as Pie-way 60. Among Kathy's many scrumptious offerings is this blend of New Mexico pecans with oats, which cuts the pie's characteristic sweetness a bit while enhancing the nutty crunch. Until Kathy suggested that it's nearly as easy to make two pies as just one, the idea of such a pie largess never occurred to us. Freeze the second for up to a month or send home slices with friends. Believe us, you'll find something to do with it. We suggest a superbly flaky lard-and-butter crust for this, but use any pie shell that you like.

Makes 2 pies

Pie crust

2½ cups all-purpose flour

1½ teaspoons salt

½ cup unsalted butter, well chilled, cut in small cubes

½ cup lard, well chilled

6 to 8 tablespoons ice water

Filling

¾ cup sugar

½ cup unsalted butter, softened

1 teaspoon ground cinnamon

¼ to ½ teaspoon ground cloves

½ teaspoon salt

1 cup light Karo syrup

1 cup dark Karo syrup or cane syrup

6 large eggs

1 cup old-fashioned oats (not quick cooking)

2 cups toasted pecan pieces

toasted pecan halves

For the pie crust

1. Pour flour and salt into a food processor and pulse together. Scatter the butter over the flour and pulse quickly several more times, just enough to submerge the butter. Scatter spoonfuls of lard over the flour-butter mixture and pulse again quickly several more times until it disappears into the flour, too. Sprinkle in 3 tablespoons of water, pulse again, then add 3 more tablespoons of water and pulse once more.

2. Dump the mixture onto a pastry board. Lightly rub the dough with your fingers. If it doesn't yet hold together when you compact it with your fingers, add another 1 or 2 tablespoons of water, as needed. Pat the dough together lightly, divide it in half, and pat each half into a fat disk. Wrap each half of the dough in plastic and refrigerate for at least 30 minutes.

3. Roll out the first chilled dough disk on a floured surface into a thin round 1 or 2 inches larger than the pie pan. Arrange crust in a greased pie pan, avoiding stretching it. Crimp the edge, then refrigerate it for at least 15 additional minutes. Line a second pie pan with the second crust.

For the filling and pie

1. Preheat the oven to 350° F.

2. Cream sugar and butter in a mixer over medium speed until the sugar has dissolved. Add the spices and salt and mix well. Stop the mixer and pour in both syrups. Mix at medium-low speed. Add the eggs, one at a time. Stop the mixer and stir in the oats by hand.

3. Scatter ½ of the pecan pieces in the bottom of each pie shell. Pour ½ of the filling into each pie shell, arranging pecan halves on top as you wish. Bake for 45 minutes, then check to see if the pies still jiggle at the center. If they have more than a very slight movement, bake them a few more minutes. Do not overbake. The pies will set up as they cool.

4. Let the pies cool for at least 1 hour before slicing into wedges and serving.

Working ahead: Pie crusts, in the pie pans, can be covered and frozen for up to a month. Fill and bake without thawing. The pie can be baked a day ahead of serving. As mentioned above, the pie freezes well, too.

Edith Warner's Chocolate Cake

Dr. Frances Levine, director of the New Mexico History Museum, started the quest. "You'll want to include Edith Warner's chocolate cake in the cookbook," Fran suggested, with a look of anticipation in her eyes. It sounded like a good idea and an easy one to fulfill. After all, Miss Warner and her tearoom, just down "the hill" from Los Alamos, both figured prominently into the lore of the atomic bomb's development in the mountains of New Mexico during World War II. We found a recipe quickly in Peggy Pond Church's biography of Edith Warner, *The House at Otowi Bridge* (1973), but it turned out like an oven-baked adobe brick. Seeking help from friends, we consulted Claire Ulam Weiner and Ellen Bradbury Reid, whose fathers were involved in the Manhattan Project. Along with Françoise Ulam (Claire's mother), Betty Lilienthal, and Nancy Meem Wirth, they tracked down another recipe, which Sharon Snyder at the Los Alamos Historical Society compared with a handwritten version in the society's files and verified as accurate. For all the difficulty in finding the right directions, it's a simple cake to master, one that requires no special occasion except a cup of tea or a frosty glass of milk. Edith Warner apparently used a loaf pan for making the cake, and you certainly can too by adding a couple of minutes to the baking time. We find the cake more attractive, though, when prepared in a round pan and sliced in wedges. The instructions assume you're baking at sea level, but they require only minor tweaking to adjust for high-altitude cooking. For example, at our 7,000-foot elevation at home we decrease the baking powder to 1 teaspoon and increase the milk by 1 tablespoon.

Serves 8

Cake

1 cup unbleached all-purpose flour

1¼ teaspoons baking powder

½ teaspoon salt

1½ ounces Baker's unsweetened chocolate, chopped

3 tablespoons unsalted butter

1 cup granulated sugar

½ cup whole milk

3 large eggs

Icing

1¼ cups confectioners' sugar

2 heaping tablespoons cocoa

pinch of salt

2 tablespoons unsalted butter, melted

2 to 3 tablespoons coffee

Raised in Pennsylvania, Edith Warner moved to New Mexico in 1922 and settled in a small adobe cottage overlooking the Rio Grande at a spot known as Otowi Crossing. Her house stood next to the single-lane suspension bridge over the river on Highway 502 that led to San Ildefonso Pueblo, a short drive away, and then up the foothills of the Jemez Mountains to Los Alamos, which at the time was nothing more than the site of a boy's prep school.

To support herself, Edith opened a teahouse in the front parlor of her home, serving the few travelers who happened by. The clientele changed dramatically in nature and numbers after 1943, when the U.S. government secretly purchased Los Alamos for the Manhattan Project to pursue its race with the Germans to develop an atomic bomb. Edith's place, already famous for its chocolate cake, became the off-duty hangout for the scientists and military officers working up the road. As Ellen Bradbury Reid remembers it from her childhood, the adults gathered on the front porch or in the parlor, the kids played outside, and Edith—wearing the white leggings of the nearby Pueblo women—quietly served everyone without asking pesky questions. Project director Robert Oppenheimer wanted his research team kept happy, so he allowed the demure Edith access to the commissary's chocolate and butter, otherwise highly rationed at the time.

For the cake

1. Preheat the oven to 250° F. Grease and flour an 8-inch round cake pan.

2. Sift together the flour, baking powder, and salt. Melt the chocolate with the butter in a small heavy pan over low heat. Pour the sugar into a mixing bowl and pour the melted chocolate over it. Combine the mixture until grainy with an electric mixer. (Edith used the rotary eggbeater more common to her generation.) Stop the mixer. Add the flour mixture and milk and beat for 1 minute, during which the batter will lighten considerably in color and texture. Stop the mixer and scrape down the sides of the bowl. Add eggs and beat for about 1 more minute, until the batter increases in volume a bit and holds its shape like softly whipped cream. Spoon the batter into the prepared pan and smooth the top.

3. Bake the cake for about 1 hour total. After 15 minutes, raise the heat to 275° F and after another 15 minutes, raise the heat to 300° F. Continue baking at 300° F about 30 minutes more, until a toothpick inserted into the cake comes out with just the barest crumb attached. Place the pan on a baking rack to cool approximately 20 minutes. Run a knife around the inside edge of the pan to loosen the cake and unmold it. Turn it back so that the top side is up and let it cool completely.

For the icing

1. Sift together the confectioners' sugar, cocoa, and salt into a mixing bowl. Add butter and mix with a whisk or electric mixer. Pour in 2 tablespoons of coffee and beat, then add just enough more coffee so that the frosting has a shiny, easily spreadable consistency.

Assembly

1. Place the cake on a serving platter. Ice the cake, ideally using an offset-handled spatula. There's enough icing to give a thorough but rather thin coat to the top and sides. Slice into wedges and serve.

Working ahead: The cake keeps well for another day. Let the frosting set before covering it. Seal well but try to keep the plastic from rubbing the cake's top directly.

10 Snacks and Party Nibbles

Maybe the New Mexico fondness for little treats goes back to the *meriendas* of the past, the afternoon teas with snacks that were popular in many Hispano cultures. Or perhaps it's a function of the extended-family gatherings that occur so frequently in the state for holidays, weddings, religious rites, and more. Or it could be just about hunger.

Whatever the case, New Mexicans love an array of nibbles and finger foods, particularly when family or friends get together in celebration, commiseration, or simple good cheer. Sometimes the refreshments will be sweets, such as the empanaditas and biscochitos in the dessert chapter, but there will certainly be savory items as well, like the ones we're serving here.

A Trio of New Mexico Nuts

New Mexico seems to grow nuttier every year. Originally we only had pine nuts, harvested by Native Americans from indigenous piñon trees. Then farmers in the Mesilla Valley and other fertile areas nearby began raising pecans, eventually producing more in some years than any other state. In one of the pecan regions, the Tularosa Basin, George and Marianne Schweer took a path less traveled in 1974, planting an alternative crop of pistachio trees, which now number some twelve thousand on their family ranch alone. Any one of these nuts tastes great on their own, but serving the three together in separate bowls (not mixed) provides a delightful contrast in flavors and textures. We roast the piñons simply, leaving you or your guests to shell them by hand. The Sassy Pecans and Christmas Pistachios share an unhidden secret, a dusting of red chile. Preparing all three takes more time than making a dip for chips, but it's triply satisfying.

Oven-Roasted Piñon Nuts

unshelled piñon nuts

1. Preheat oven to 300° F.

2. Place unshelled nuts on a rimmed baking sheet. Bake for 50 to 60 minutes, stirring every 10 minutes or so to allow the nuts to toast evenly. Cool, mound into a bowl, and crack open with fingers. People have traditionally done this with their teeth, but that's a good way to end up with an unplanned visit to the dentist. If you don't intend to eat the piñons within a few days, store them in the refrigerator or freezer. They will keep longer than when shelled, up to a year.

Sassy Pecans

Makes 2 cups

2 cups pecan halves

½ cup confectioners' sugar

1 teaspoon ground dried
   New Mexico red chile

½ teaspoon salt, or more to taste

New Mexico Peanuts

You can also prepare New Mexico peanuts in much the same way as the pistachios, merely substituting peanut oil for the butter. You won't then have a quartet of nuts, however, because technically peanuts are legumes, more like peas than nuts.

Much of the country's organic peanut crop comes from the arid eastern plains of New Mexico, in Portales and surrounding Roosevelt County. The lack of humidity and the sandy soil make it easier to avoid molds and critters without resorting to the fungicides and pesticides used elsewhere. In the fall, after the peanuts are harvested from underground, they are allowed to dry in the strong sun.

1. Preheat the oven to 350° F. Line a baking sheet with parchment paper. Rinse the pecans in just enough water to wet all of the nuts, then drain.

2. Combine the confectioners' sugar, red chile, and salt in a bowl. Add the pecans and toss together. Dump the pecans out onto the baking sheet.

3. Bake 10 to 12 minutes, until the sugar has caramelized lightly. Mound into a bowl and eat warm or at room temperature. Pecans can be kept in a sealed jar at room temperature for several weeks. For longer storage, freeze the nuts.

Christmas Pistachios

Makes 2 cups

1 tablespoon unsalted butter

2 cups (about 8 ounces) roasted
   unsalted pistachios

1 to 1½ teaspoons ground dried
   New Mexican red chile

½ teaspoon salt, or more to taste

1. Warm the oil in a large skillet over medium heat. Stir in the pistachios, coating them on all sides with butter. Sprinkle in the chile and ½ teaspoon of salt, adding more if you wish after tasting.

2. Dump the pistachios onto absorbent paper to cool. Mound into a bowl or seal tightly in a jar to keep for up to several weeks at room temperature.

Pepitas

Pumpkin seed kernels, known as *pepitas* in New Mexico and other Hispano lands, are something of a bonus food, cast off by the unsuspecting when carving Halloween jack-o'-lanterns. The term "pepita", or "little seed," can refer to the whole seed, but it's typically used to describe the greenish kernel of meat hidden inside the large creamy-colored pod. While they are readily available from commercial sources, you can also collect your own and take pride in making use of something that most folks discard. Plan to bake the pumpkin itself for eating now or later. It can be pureed and bagged for the freezer, where it keeps well for months. You can also treat a large winter squash in the same fashion.

Makes approximately ½ cup

1 medium to large pumpkin

about 1 tablespoon vegetable oil

salt

1. Preheat the oven to 400° F. Arrange parchment paper on the baking sheet.

2. Cut the pumpkin open either from the top, jack-o'-lantern style, or simply slice it in two halves avoiding the stem. With a sturdy large spoon, scrape out the seeds and stringy, goopy pulp at the core. Place the seeds in a bowl and rinse them with your fingers to separate them from the pulp. This may take a couple of rinses. Save the pumpkin itself for another use.

3. Combine the seeds with enough oil just to coat them on the baking sheet. Bake for 20 to 25 minutes, until slightly colored and crisp. Set aside to cool.

4. Crack the seeds open with your fingers to yield the kernels inside. When all the seeds are shelled, salt the kernels and eat.

Working ahead: Store pepitas in an airtight container in the freezer if you're not eating them right away. Like piñon nuts, they go rancid easily because of their high fat content.

Jícama with Lime and Chile

When Bill first moved to Tesuque and his daughter Heather started second grade at the neighborhood school, the teacher assigned the students to bring various vegetables to class for a discussion. She gave Heather the task of securing a jícama, which Bill figured was a test to see if the new Anglo knew the locally popular tuber from a plain old turnip. As we've looked back on the experience, which was long before the current efforts to get kids enthusiastic about fresh food, we've realized the lesson inspired all of us to enjoy the homely jícama's crisp refreshing sweetness more often than we would have otherwise.

Serves a party

1 jícama (they range quite a bit in size and in shape—from a small ball to a misshapen football)

1 cucumber, optional

lime wedges

salt, optional

ground dried red New Mexican chile

1. Cut off the jícama's fibrous brown skin with a paring knife and discard it. Cut the white flesh of the jícama into manageable sections, then cut into slices ¼ to ½ inch thick. If using the cucumber, slice into rounds of similar thickness.

2. Arrange the jícama slices on a plate or platter, interspersing them with the optional cucumber. Squeeze lime juice over the slices generously and sprinkle with salt (optional) and chile. Alternatively, serve the chile in a small bowl on the side, for dunking the slices.

A Land of Contrasts

What is New Mexico, then? How sum it up? It is a vast, harsh, poverty-stricken, varied, and beautiful land, a breeder of artists and warriors. It is the home, by birth or passionate adoption, of a wildly assorted population which has shown itself capable of achieving homogeneity without sacrificing its diversity. It is primitive, undeveloped, overused, new, raw, rich with tradition, old, and mellow.

—OLIVER LA FARGE, "NEW MEXICO," *HOLIDAY* MAGAZINE (1952)

Tortilla Pinwheels

Google "tortilla pinwheels" today and you'll find hundreds of variations of a party tidbit that has been popular here since at least the 1970s. Sure, you can wrap a tortilla around just about anything, but New Mexico remains partial to its own elemental version featuring chopped green chile and cream cheese. No one can eat just one.

Makes about 24 pinwheels

8 ounces cream cheese (a lower fat version is fine here), softened

1 garlic clove, minced, optional

4 thin 8-inch flour tortillas, at room temperature

¾ cup chopped roasted New Mexican green chile, fresh or thawed frozen, well drained

salsa, optional

1. Stir the cream cheese until light and smooth, adding the garlic if you like.

2. Spread the cream cheese over the tortillas. Scatter each tortilla evenly with the green chile. Roll up the tortillas snugly. Wrap them in plastic or wax paper, twisting the ends, and refrigerate for at least 1 hour and up to 12 hours.

3. Unwrap and cut off about ½ inch from the ends of each tortilla. (Cook's treat.) Cut the tortillas into slices, about ¾ inch thick, with a sharp knife.

4. Plate the pinwheels, cut side up. Let them sit covered at room temperature for a few minutes before serving, with salsa if you wish.

Variations: Don't fancy these up too much, but you can consider an addition or two from items such as shredded cheddar, well-drained black beans, roasted corn kernels, onion, cilantro, scallions, chopped green or black olives, ham, or bits of crisp bacon. Scatter a scant amount of each over the tortillas before the chile goes on.

New Mexico Cheese

It surprises most people to learn that New Mexico is one of the country's top dairy-producing states, with the eighth largest cheese industry. Of our scores of dairies, nearly a third of them are in the Chaves County area surrounding Roswell. Most are family owned but often have more than a thousand head of cattle. Milk is typically sold to cooperatives and then turned into commodity cheese.

The Tucumcari Mountain Cheese Factory is a midsize operation, which brings in milk from a New Mexico farmers' cooperative. It makes a fine feta and has a Native Pastures line of organic cheeses, found now in a growing number of supermarkets.

Several smaller producers make cheeses from the milk of their own herd, meaning their hand-crafted artisan products can be classified as farmstead cheeses. Coonridge Organic Goat Cheese, preserved in olive oil and sold in jars, is made from the milk of Nancy Coonridge's free-ranging goats near Pie Town. She was named New Mexico's 2009 Organic Farmer of the Year. South Mountain Dairy near Edgewood also makes farmstead goat cheeses. Some are in French styles, but their *queso* Lizette is like

Fresh Goat Cheese with Green Chile Chutney

This chutney evolved from a recipe in Lucy Delgado's important 1979 book *Comidas de New Mexico*. She liked the relish, as she called it, with hamburgers, hot dogs, and meat loaf, but it also makes a splendid accompaniment to the simple cheeses once made regularly at home.

the basic *queso de cabra* made here in generations past. Typically, it is sliced and served with honey, cane syrup, or molasses. Sweetwoods Dairy, in Peña Blanca, started its business with creamy fresh goat cheeses, including *requesón*, but has been focused more recently on aged cheeses such as their luscious Tazon de Lanto goat-and-sheep cheese, aged sixty days; it reminds us of Manchego. The Old Windmill Dairy near Estancia makes some farmstead cheeses and some from neighbors' milk, all in small batches. Some of the cheeses are now cave-aged. Look for these and other small producers selling their cheeses at farmers' markets and sometimes in co-ops and a few other specialty shops as well.

Serves 6 or more

Green Chile Chutney

¾ cup cider or white vinegar

¾ cup sugar

½ medium onion, minced

½ teaspoon yellow mustard seed

¼ teaspoon salt

pinch of ground cumin

1½ cups chopped roasted New Mexican green chile, fresh or defrosted frozen

10 to 12 ounces creamy fresh goat cheese, preferably New Mexican, softened

crackers

For the chutney

1. Combine the vinegar, sugar, onion, mustard seed, salt, and cumin in a saucepan and bring to a boil over high heat. Reduce the heat to a simmer and cook for 10 minutes. Stir in the green chile and continue cooking for about 10 minutes longer, until thickened and jammy. Cool.

Assembly

1. Either pour the chutney over the cheese or serve it in a bowl on a platter with the cheese. Accompany with the crackers.

Working ahead: The chutney can be made up to 2 weeks ahead if spooned into a sterilized jar and refrigerated.

Chile con Queso

Until the two of us arrived in New Mexico, we thought of chile con queso as a Velveeta cheese dip of little real interest. Bell Mondragon, an accomplished home cook turned chef-restaurateur, taught us differently. Bell and her husband, Roberto, the former lieutenant governor of the state and a noted musician, reside in Cuyamungue, but she used to serve the dish in this style at both Maria Ysabel and Comicalla, the popular restaurants she operated in Santa Fe. (The latter was named as a play on the expression "*Come y calla*," which means "Shut up and eat.") We have since found similar versions, once Bell inspired us to look, some of which refer to the dish as chile verde con queso.

Serves 4 or more

1 cup green chile sauce (page 26) or other mild green chile sauce

¼ to ½ cup chicken stock

6 ounces (¾ cup) shredded Monterey Jack cheese

tortilla chips or wedges of warm flour tortillas

1. Bring the green chile sauce and stock to a boil in a heavy saucepan. If the sauce is fairly thick, use the full amount of stock. Otherwise, start with the smaller amount. Sprinkle in the cheese and quickly cover the pan. Remove from the heat and let stand 2 to 3 minutes. Uncover and stir the mixture to combine. Add a bit more stock if the mixture seems overly thick.

2. Serve immediately, kept heated on a warming tray if you like. Accompany with chips or tortilla wedges.

Variations: Many cheeses don't work well in this dish. Out of Monterey Jack and in the mood for chile con queso, we once used a combination of queso Oaxaca and cheddar, figuring the mild buttery Oaxacan would balance out the slightly firmer and stronger cheddar. It was a disaster of strings and globs. Queso Oaxaca is in the same family of cheeses as mozzarella, meaning it is meant to pull into strings, so it didn't blend into the liquid. Cheddar is in a category of cheeses firmer than semi-soft Monterey Jack and did not melt nearly as well in liquid. Our attempts to stir it more aggressively to blend the cheese just made the ugly situation worse.

Homemade Tortilla Chips

Before every convenience store in the country carried a lifetime supply of packaged tortilla chips, New Mexican cooks made their own. Doing that yourself for the chile con queso really turns it into a signature creation.

Cut corn tortillas (page 137) into pie-slice quarters. Pour vegetable oil or even old-fashioned lard into a broad and moderately deep pan to a depth of several inches and heat to 400° F. Fry as many tortilla wedges as fit comfortably in the pan, just until they turn crisp, a matter of seconds. Drain and salt them right away. If you've taken the time to do this, be sure to serve the chips warm.

Summer Avocado Dip

Sara Howell, a twentysomething home cook born and raised in Albuquerque, proudly shared the recipe for this fresh vegetable dip made out of the first harvest from her newly planted organic garden. The garden survived drought and a new puppy, but the initial pickings were a bit skimpy. She decided to put everything together with a couple of avocados, and this was the result. In following Sara's lead, feel free to use the same sense of discovery that inspired her. This differs from guacamole in that the avocado here is simply a binder for the wealth of vegetables and herbs.

Makes about 3 cups

1 cup diced tomatoes, preferably a combination of red and yellow varieties

½ to 1 leek, white portion only, sliced very thin

2 to 3 chopped peppers or chiles, preferably a combination of banana peppers with New Mexican green chile

1 tablespoon fresh dill, minced

1 garlic clove, minced

2 large ripe avocados (preferably Haas variety), chunked

juice of ½ lemon

few dashes of hot sauce, optional

salt

tortilla chips or other chips or crackers, or crisp vegetables

1. In a large bowl, stir together the tomatoes, leek, peppers, dill, and garlic. Add the avocados, mashing roughly, leaving some small chunks. Stir in the remaining ingredients, adding optional hot sauce and salt to taste.

2. Serve within about 30 minutes with chips, crackers, or vegetables.

11 *Beverages*

New Mexicans make some of the best margaritas in the Southwest and play the role of guardian angel in preserving historic corn-based drinks in the region, but the state hasn't staked a claim to many special beverages of its own. That could happen in the next few decades with the recent revival of small-scale wineries, breweries, and even distilleries dedicated to blending signature products, but for now New Mexicans tend to excel in preparation techniques rather than innovation.

We've certainly had spurts of creativity over time. Native Americans, early settlers, and later herbalists harvested the abundant wild herbs of the area to make teas and tisanes, including the *cota*, or Indian tea, still consumed today. Generations of Hispanic mothers and grandmothers have calmed children or colicky babies with *alhucema*, a lavender tisane. In the mountain-man period of the first half of the nineteenth century, distilleries thrived in northern New Mexico, fabricating Taos Lightning, which was shipped around the West. Home cooks mixed their own versions of *mistela de Chimajá*, infusing whiskey with sweet spices, and *tesquino*, a corn beer.

These drinks of old have lost ground or disappeared entirely as similar or more refined commercial products have become widely available. The heritage of experimentation and homegrown mixology is likely more dormant than dead, however, and may once again bloom in the future.

Classic Margarita

Probably first concocted across New Mexico's southern border in Ciudad Juárez, the margarita is the specialty cocktail of the state, widely popular and made in many masterful versions. Maria's in Santa Fe, in particular, staked a claim to margarita excellence long before the current craze for fine bar drinks. Owners Al and Laurie Lucero, actively involved with the café's food and drink, offer more than 170 solid variations, many of which appeared in Al's best-selling *The Great Margarita Book* (2003). Al is adamant, as we are, that a margarita should be made in a cocktail shaker so that just enough ice melts to enhance the drink's proportions. Then it should be served straight up or on the rocks. Al points out that while all Cointreau is triple sec, not all triple sec is Cointreau. You get what you pay for. And many folks here believe that lemon juice makes a better margarita than lime because it has a more consistent flavor and blends rather than contrasts with the taste of a good tequila. Don't bother with an expensive sipping tequila for margaritas, but insist on one that is 100 percent agave.

Serves 1

fresh lemon or lime wedge

coarse salt

cracked ice

2 ounces premium silver tequila

1 ounce Cointreau

1 ounce fresh lemon juice

1. Rub a lemon or lime wedge around the rim of an 8-ounce glass. Place a thin layer of salt on a saucer and dip the lime-rubbed rim of the glass into the salt.

2. Fill a cocktail shaker or similar-size lidded jar with cracked ice. Pour the tequila, Cointreau, and lemon juice into the container and shake to blend. Strain the margarita into the prepared glass and serve.

Variations: We're ignoring the numerous fruity, syrupy snow-cone confections often palmed off as margaritas. You should, too. If you want a little more color, Maria's offers one with a blood orange base. For some retro fun, opt for turquoise margaritas made with blue curaçao at Maria's or other spots. In Mesilla, the Double Eagle offers a turquoise margarita that comes with a chunk of New Mexican turquoise as a take-home souvenir. La Posta de Mesilla's Chile 'Rita combines in a shaker with 1½ ounces of Sauza Hornitos tequila, ½ ounce of Cointreau, 2 ounces sweet-and-sour mix, ½ ounce fresh-squeezed lime juice, and ½ ounce Besito Caliente, a blackberry-habanero sauce created by the Truck Farm in Las Cruces and available online (www.sweethots.com).

Chope's Bar & Café

José "Chope" Benavides was born in the nineteenth-century house that became his namesake restaurant, and his widowed wife, Lupe, still lives there behind the dining rooms. Their three daughters oversee daily operations today. Chope's takes the concept of a family business to the ultimate level.

It all started around 1915 when Longina Benavides, Chope's mother, began selling enchiladas to Mesilla Valley farmers near the small town of La Mesa. She notified patrons about the availability of food by hanging a kerosene lantern outside her front door. When Longina died, Lupe continued the tradition, and Chope added a bar where he presided with an engaging smile, wit, and major political clout.

Cool down with a margarita or oversize bottled beer while you consider the hearty options. The menu today extends well beyond enchiladas, but it still features fabulous home cooking in the southern New Mexico style. It's hard to go wrong with any choice, but don't overlook the famed chile rellenos, which inspired Chope to coin the restaurant's slogan, "Stuff It!"

Many restaurants start with some kind of vision, usually involving fortunes to be made, but Florence and Arturo Jaramillo had one of the grandest visions ever in New Mexico for Rancho de Chimayó. From the inception of the idea, they planned to make the family home of Arturo's grandparents, where he grew up as a child, into a living history museum that would demonstrate the vibrancy and vitality of the local Hispano heritage. The dream survives to this day under Florence's continuing management and sees some degree of fulfillment in every meal served.

The Jaramillos based the original menu on dishes that Arturo's grandmother prepared regularly. From the beginning the cooks were mainly Chimayó ladies who made everything like they did in their own kitchens, which resulted in slight variations from day to day depending on the woman at the stove. Even as greater consistency developed over time, the food retained a special down-home flavor.

The dining rooms convey a similar homey feeling, with old family photographs on the adobe walls and fireplaces blazing during the winter months. If it makes you want to spend the night, you can do it right across the street at the Hacienda Rancho de Chimayó, built by Arturo's great-uncle in an identical fashion to the house where you're having dinner.

Chimayó Cocktail

Apples thrive as a crop through the north-central area of the state, from Velarde and Dixon down through Peña Blanca. Farmers lost many trees in 1971 when temperatures sank well below zero, but growers replanted and have managed to produce crisp refreshing fruit in spite of drought, wind, and other travails. When the Rancho de Chimayó Restaurante opened in the 1960s, the Jaramillo family owners wanted to create a cocktail flavored with the cherished local apples. They paired it with tequila, the state's favorite spirit, and produced this wonderful result. It's still the restaurant's signature drink and popular in plenty of other establishments and at home parties as well.

Serves 1

ice cubes

1½ ounces premium gold
  tequila

1½ ounces apple cider,
  preferably unfiltered

¼ ounce fresh lemon juice

¼ ounce créme de cassis

unpeeled apple slice, for garnish

1. Half fill an 8-ounce glass with ice cubes. Pour all of the ingredients over the ice and stir to blend. Garnish the rim of the glass with the apple slice and serve.

Atole

New Mexico's all-time favorite beverage, enjoyed for centuries by Native Americans, Hispanos, and Anglos alike, atole isn't as common as it used to be, but it has plenty of devoted fans. Originally from Mexico, where it is also still found, atole seems to have disappeared over time in most of the Southwest. This is a New Mexican variation on the drink, using blue cornmeal, but otherwise it's made much like versions from elsewhere past and present. Some people say that it's an acquired taste, but if you like cornbread or polenta you may take to atole quickly.

Serves 2 or more

½ cup finely ground blue cornmeal or toasted blue cornmeal

½ cup hot water

2½ cups cold water or milk

granulated sugar or salt

milk or ground *canela* (Mexican cinnamon) or both, optional

1. Stir the cornmeal and hot water in a small bowl until they form a smooth paste.

2. Bring the cold water to a full boil. Whisk the cornmeal mixture into the hot liquid and stir constantly until it has a light thickness and the liquid no longer separates completely from the meal. Add a few teaspoons of sugar or a few pinches of salt and stir until dissolved. Continue to stir occasionally until cool enough to drink.

3. Pour into heatproof mugs and serve. Add a splash of milk if you like. If serving the atole with sugar, a dusting of cinnamon is a nice topping in each mug.

Way Before Napa Valley

Spanish authorities prohibited colonies in the New World from producing their own wine, wanting them to import it from the mother country at substantial cost. Settlers everywhere ignored the law. A Franciscan priest and Capuchin monk brought the first wine grapevine cuttings to New Mexico in 1629 and planted them on the east bank of the Rio Grande at the San Antonio de Padua Mission south of present-day Socorro. Wine production began at the mission in 1633 and supplied New Mexico's sacramental needs for the next forty years.

Around the time California missions planted the first grapes in that territory in 1769, New Mexico had strings of wineries along the Rio Grande from Bernalillo to Socorro and from the Mesilla area to El Paso (a New Mexican town then). Pre-statehood production peaked at around one million gallons annually in 1884, when New Mexico ranked fifth in the country in output thanks to the local popularity of wine. Flooding and erosion along the Rio Grande reduced grapevine acreage after that, and Prohibition killed all but a single winery making sacramental wines.

The rebirth of the industry started in 1978. New Mexico now boasts more than forty wineries and an annual production getting increasingly close to the million-gallon level again. For information on New Mexico wines, wineries, festivals, and wine touring, check out the website of the New Mexico Wine Growers Association (www.nmwine.com).

Hot Chocolate New Mexico Style

Sure, you can whip up a cup of hot chocolate in an instant, but when you really want to savor a cup, try this. Ally Sinclair, master chocolatier, offered us this fragrantly intense version for the book. She and her husband, Max, founded Cocopotamus Chocolate in Albuquerque, a small company that has already made a big impression on cacao fans in and out of the state. The Aztecs reserved chocolate beverages for Montezuma's court and the elite. A cup of this will show you why.

Serves 4 or more

2 to 3 heaping tablespoons dark Dutch-processed cocoa powder

1 pint heavy cream

1 quart whole or 2% milk

2 or 3 dried New Mexican red chiles, stemmed, seeded, and snipped or broken into several pieces each

1 teaspoon ground ginger

½ teaspoon ground cinnamon

¼ teaspoon ground cayenne

¼ teaspoon salt

4 to 5 tablespoons granulated sugar

softly whipped cream

1. Spoon the cocoa into a bowl or pitcher. Stir in the cream until the mixture is smooth. Stir in the milk, chiles, spices, and salt. Cover and refrigerate overnight or for at least 4 hours, for the flavors to infuse and mingle.

2. Pour the chocolate mixture through a strainer into a heavy saucepan. Stir in sugar to taste.

3. Warm over medium heat, stirring gently, until tiny bubbles form around the pan's edge and the chocolate is hot. Serve in mugs with whipped cream.

Variations: Sometimes New Mexican hot chocolate, like its Mexican counterpart, has an egg frothed in it by use of a wooden Mexican hand tool called a *molinillo*. A bit like a rudimentary rotary eggbeater, the *molinillo* is placed into the pot of chocolate and then rolled back and forth rapidly between the palms to whip the mixture into a thicker foamy beverage.

Agua de Sandia

Stands featuring giant glass jars brimming with Mexican-style *aguas frescas*, *limonadas*, and *liquados* have become increasingly widespread in New Mexico in recent years, but the love of fruit drinks goes back eons in human history. Watermelon, originally from Africa, arrived in New Mexico even before the Spanish, introduced by native traders bringing seeds north from Mexico. It's been one of the area's favorite fruits since that time and makes a marvelous juice. A few strawberries, a ripe peach, or a chunk of cantaloupe can be tasty and colorful additions.

Serves 6

8 cups loosely packed seeded watermelon chunks

¼ cup packed fresh mint leaves

1½ cups water or sparkling water or lemonade

sugar

mint sprigs for garnish

1. Puree the watermelon in a blender in batches, adding the ¼ cup of mint leaves to one of the batches. Pour the watermelon juice into a large pitcher. Stir in the water (or lemonade) and taste. Perfectly ripe, peak-of-the-season fruit doesn't require sugar, but add a tablespoon or more if needed to get a well-balanced sweet and fruity taste. Chill for at least 1 hour.

2. Pour over ice in tall glasses and garnish each with a mint sprig. Serve.

The Brew Craft

Beer brewing doesn't have as long a history in New Mexico as wine making, but business has been booming since 1988, when the Santa Fe Brewing Company became the state's first microbrewery. Approximately two dozen independent operations exist now, spread around the whole state but particularly concentrated in the Albuquerque area. Check out the list at www.newmexico.org/cuisine/micro-breweries.

The brewmasters in these establishments love to experiment with all types of beer, from India pale ale to Irish stout, and pilsner to porter. They also enjoy adding local accents with New Mexico ingredients, including chile of course.

Among all the fascinating brews, one of the most interesting is Monks' Ale, owned and operated by the Christ in the Desert Monastery in a remote wilderness area near Abiquiu. As one of the Benedictine brothers explains, the monastery must support itself, and monks have been funding their religious order by making and selling beer since the Middle Ages. Traditions don't die easily in New Mexico.

New Mexico Culinary Resources

New Mexican Food Products by Mail

Hatch Chile Express
657 North Franklin Street
Hatch, NM 87937
Cases of fresh chiles, in season, and frozen and dried chile
www.hatch-chile.com
575-267-3226

New Mexico's Own
Online market of made in New Mexico products
www.newmexicosown.com

Santa Fe School of Cooking & Market
125 North Guadalupe Street
Santa Fe, NM 87501
New Mexico's most extensive source for mail-order food products, supplies, and cooking equipment such as asadors and tortilla presses
www.santafeschoolofcooking.com
800-982-4688, 505-983-4511

Branded New Mexican Food Products by Mail

Bueno Foods
Sauces, salsas, dried chile
www.weshipchile.com
800-95-CHILE

Casados Farm
Dried chiles and other dried food products including hard-to-find chicos and panocha flour
505-852-2443

El Pinto
Sauces and salsas
www.elpinto.com
505-898-1771

El Rancho de Los Garcias
Sauces and salsas
www.elranchodelosgarcias.com
575-693-7296

El Rincón Farm
True Chimayó chile from the farm
elrinconfarm@gmail.com
505-577-4349

Los Chileros de Nuevo Mexico
Sauces, salsas, dried chiles, and other
dried New Mexico food products
www.888eatchile.com
888-Eat-CHILE

North of the Border
Artisanal sauces, salsas, dried chiles, and
condiments
www.northoftheborder.net
505-982-0681

The Shed
Sauces, dried chiles, and other dried
food products, including hard to find
New Mexico green chiles
www.theshedsantafe.com
505-982-0982

The Truck Farm/Desert Farms
New Mexico condiments
www.sweethots.com
800-A1-HONEY, 575-523-1447

~~~~~~~~~~~
Places to Experience New Mexico's Living Culinary Heritage

El Rancho de Las Golondrinas
La Cienega, south of Santa Fe
www.golondrinas.org

Los Poblanos de Albuquerque Inn &
Cultural Center (and farm)
Los Ranchos de Albuquerque
Open just for scheduled events.
www.lospoblanos.com

New Mexico Farm & Ranch Heritage
Museum,
Las Cruces
www.nmfarmandranchmuseum.org

~~~~~~~~~~~
Seeds and Plants by Mail

High Country Gardens
Native plants, xeric perennials, and
other edible plants selected for New
Mexico
www.highcountrygardens.com
800-925-9387, 505-438-3031

Native Seeds/SEARCH
Seeds for many hard to find traditional
crops of New Mexico and the Southwest
www.nativeseeds.org
520-622-0830

~~~~~~~~~~~
High-Altitude Cooking Tips

For a printout (Guide E-215) from
New Mexico State University's
County Extension Service
http://cahedev.nmsu/pubs/_e/E-215.pdf

~~~~~~~~~~~
Statewide Culinary Information

New Mexico Tourism Department
www.newmexico.org/cuisine

New Mexico Farmers' Marketing
Association
www.farmersmarketsnm.com

New Mexico Wine Growers
Association
www.nmwine.com

New Mexico Culinary Publications

Edible Santa Fe, from Taos to Albuquerque
www.ediblecommunities.com/santafe

LocalFlavor
www.localflavormagazine.com

The Zenchilada
www.zenchilada.com

Statewide Restaurant Reviews

From Gil Garduño, with an emphasis on traditional foods
www.nmgastronome.com

Food Events and Meet-Ups

Homegrown New Mexico
Produces events that promote the benefits of homegrown and home-preserved foods and keeps a calendar of culinary activities
www.homegrownnewmexico.com

Slow Food
Middle Rio Grande Chapter:
www.slowfoodriogrande.org
Santa Fe Chapter:
http://slowfoodsantafe.blogspot.com

New Mexico Centennial and Legacy Project Information

www.nmcentennial.org

Acknowledgments

We obviously owe an enormous debt to the people of New Mexico, past and present, for sustaining us in this project. They did all the hard work of shaping the culinary legacy we discuss.

In particular we want to thank the many people who responded to our publisher's invitation to submit recipes and stories about food in New Mexico. Some are mentioned by name in the book, others contributed passion anonymously. We're grateful to all of you.

We must also recognize the initial enablers, the people who got the cogs in motion. Restaurateur and tourism commissioner Al Lucero made an early suggestion for a cookbook as a part of the centennial celebration. Stuart Ashman, former secretary of the New Mexico Department of Cultural Affairs, immediately grasped the opportunity the book offered, as did Museum of New Mexico Press publisher Anna Gallegos. The New Mexico Centennial Foundation, under the guidance of Jodi Delaney, put their imprimatur and resources behind the book in its infancy as well.

Our friend Dr. Frances Levine, director of the New Mexico History Museum, became an early advocate and informal adviser to the project. The research and writings—as well as friendship—of ethnobotanist William Dunmire and his wife, Vangie, made our work enormously easier. Thank you, Bill and Vangie. Dr. Paul W. Bosland, regents professor and director of the Chile Pepper Institute, College of Agriculture and Home Economics, at New Mexico State University played a similarly valuable role over many years. Staff at El Rancho de las Golondrinas, Hacienda de los Martinez, Los Poblanos Inn & Cultural Center, Museum of Indian Arts and Culture, Museum of Spanish Colonial Art, New Mexico Farm and Ranch Heritage Museum, the Pueblo Indian Cultural Center, and the Santa Fe Public Library always found answers to our queries. Travis and Sacheen Suazo and Tweety and Norman Suazo gave us insights into numerous Pueblo traditions, past and present.

Tracey Ryder and Carol Topalian, founders of Edible Communities, made us feel confident that we could do justice to this subject. Ana Pacheco, founder and publisher of *La Herencia*, a journal highlighting Hispanic culture, graciously offered access to her years of issues and helped us track down some important sources. Other publishers in a variety of media, including Gwyneth Doland, Gil Garduño, Patty Karlovitz, Kate Manchester, and Pat West-Barker, have generously shared their resources with us.

Restaurateurs Florence Jaramillo and Arturo Jaramillo, along with publisher Bruce Shaw, gave us our first opportunity to write in depth about New Mexican food some two decades ago. Like the Jaramillos, Santa Fe School of Cooking owner Susan Curtis believed in us early on and gave us the opportunity to refine our understanding of the local cuisine and its practitioners, as has her daughter Nicole Curtis-Ammerman. Fellow authors, including Stan Crawford, Lois Ellen Frank, Stephen Fried, Deborah Madison, Gary Nabhan, Carmella Padilla, Marc Simmons, and Margaret Wood have fueled our passions for the food and culture of New Mexico and the Southwest. Food authorities Jennifer Fresquez, Denise Miller, Mark Miller, Bob Ross, Pam Roy, Lynn Walters, and Walter Whitewater have pointed us in the right direction many times and, like the aforementioned authors, have provided hours of engaging conversations regarding the importance of truly good food in all our lives.

Growers at the Santa Fe, Pojoaque, Taos, and Los Alamos farmers' markets have provided advice and great food to us in such quantity over so many years that we simply can't mention all of their names here. Know that we are in awe of you and your fellow farmers throughout the state. You create nothing short of modern alchemy, bringing forth gorgeous, nutritious food from "dirt" initially more suitable as building blocks. Former past and present staff members of New Mexico's Department of Agriculture, Dennis Hogan, David Lucero, and Benjie Segovia, and the staff and board of the New Mexico Beef Council helped us with background on farming and ranching. Olivia DeCamp of the New Mexico Wine Growers Association tuned us in to specifics of the state's wine industry. Ana Baca and Emma Jean Cervantes, in particular, gave us insights into the big business of chile. Ken Bowling, Chris Faivre, Tom and Jerean Hutchinson, Andrea Lawrence, Adrian "Ace" Perez, and Bobby Perez all contributed to our knowledge of the food traditions of southern New Mexico. Just about everything else we needed to know about anything else New Mexican came from Martín Leger, one of the state Tourism Department's finest ambassadors.

Doe Coover, our longtime agent and friend, continued to provide savvy advice and assistance. Museum of New Mexico Press editorial director Mary Wachs oversaw the manuscript and its production with the help of Karla Eoff and David Skolkin. Thank you for creating a beautiful book worthy of our state's milestone commemoration.

Happy Birthday, New Mexico, the state we have been fortunate to call home for more than thirty years each.

I am glad to give you life, I hope that you will be healthy.
—PRESIDENT WILLIAM H. TAFT, UPON SIGNING THE LEGISLATION TO MAKE NEW MEXICO THE FORTY-SEVENTH STATE IN THE UNITED STATES, ON SATURDAY, JANUARY 6, 1912, 1:35 p.m.

General Index

Shed, The (Santa Fe), 74, 188
Sheep, 9, 11, 13, 57, 144, 155
"shepherd's fireplace," 34
Shepherd's Lamb (Tierra Amarilla), 57, 70
Shiprock, NM, 125
Shohko Café (Santa Fe), 122
Shrove Tuesday, 39
Sikh community, 82
Silver City Food Co-op (Silver City), 91
Simply Simpático (Junior League), 33, 97, 139
Sinclair, Ally and Max, 185
Sisters of Loretto, 86, 155
Snyder, Sharon, 168
Socorro, NM, 11, 104, 184
South Mountain Dairy (Edgewood), 176
Southeast Asia, 30
Spain, 9–11, 42, 53, 144, 149, 150, 156
Spanish colonial folk crafts, 14
Spanish explorers, 22, 86
Spanish Pueblo architecture, 14
Spanish settlers, 29
 and beverages, 53, 181, 184
 and bread, 135, 138
 hunted game, 103, 108
 introduced chiles, 19–20
 introduced sheep, 9, 11, 57
 introduced various foods, 9–11, 47, 53, 79, 104
 in New Mexico, 9–13
 and sweets, 149, 154
State cookie, 150
State question, 19
Statehood, 14–15, 38, 46, 73, 108, 112
Suazo, Travis and Sasheen, 164
Suazo, Tweety and Norm, 164
Sunland Park, NM, 125
Sunset magazine, 77
Sweetwoods Dairy (Peña Blanca), 176

Tamalada, 79
Taos, NM, 11, 34, 71, 140
Territorial period, 13–14, 20, 64
Tesuque, NM, 44, 175
Tesuque Pueblo, 164
Texas, 11, 13, 17, 19, 54, 92, 108, 110, 151
Thanksgiving, 91, 124
Tia Sophia's (Santa Fe), 35
Tiede, Dennis, 82
Tierra Amarilla, NM, 70
Tierra Wools, 57
Tipton, Alice Stevens, 14, 45, 54, 105
Tortugas Pueblo, 42–43
Tourism, 112–13
Trade/Traders, 11–13, 34, 108, 122, 186
Traditional cooking/dishes
 Asian influence on, 97, 122
 firsthand accounts of, 12–13, 29, 44, 73
 history of, 34, 37, 41, 138
 Mexican influence on, 12–13, 73, 79, 94, 96, 122, 185

NM reverence for, 10, 150
 Pueblo influence on, 164
 Spanish influence on, 53, 79, 88, 103–04, 140, 149, 154, 156, 159
Trillin, Calvin, 35, 128
Truchas Mountain Café, 142
Truck Farm (Las Cruces), 182, 188
Trujillo, Maria Lucia and Lucaria "Carrie," 158
Tse-Pe, Dora, 119
Tucumcari Mountain Cheese Factory, 176
Tularosa Basin, NM, 172
Turner, Ted, 108

Ulam, Françoise, 168
United States Army, 13, 144
United States Patent and Trademark Office, 68
United World College, 112
Uranium Café (Grants), 34

Valencia County Chamber of Commerce, 59
Valerio, Anita, 140
Valerio, Candido, 37, 140–41
Valles Caldera National Preserve, 147
Vargas, Diego de, 11
Vaughn, NM, 113
Velarde, NM, 20, 183
Villa de San Felipe de Albuquerque, 105. *See also* Albuquerque, NM

Wagon Mound, NM, 127
Wallace, Lew, 64
Wang, Chichi, 150
Warner, Edith, 168
Washington, DC, 13
Washington Post, The, 136
We Fed Them Cactus (Gilbert), 87, 159
Weaving, 57
Weiner, Claire Ulam, 168
West Indies, 22
West Las Vegas High School, 58
Whitewater, Walter, 148
Whole Enchilada Fiesta (Las Cruces), 76
Wineries, 181, 184
Wirth, Nancy Meem, 168
Women farmers, 28, 64, 86, 125
Wood, Margaret, 48–49
Wool, 11, 34, 57
World War II, 15, 70, 147, 168
Writers, 14. *See also* specific names

Younis, Rita, 88

Zamora, Arik and Eloy, 71
Zuni Pueblo, 131, 142

Recipe
Index